The ABCs of Dating

Brenda A. Lewis, LCSW

New York, New York

© Brenda A. Lewis, LCSW, 2013
The ABCs of Dating: A Guide to Love and Dating for the Openhearted

First Printing, US 2013

ISBN: 978-0-9882250-3-9

Copyright © 2013 by Brenda A. Lewis, LCSW. Printed in the United States of America. Except as permitted under the United States Copyright Act of 1976, no part of this publication may be reproduced or distributed in any form or by any means, or stored in a database or retrieval system, without the prior written permission of the publisher.

The information contained in this book is intended to provide helpful and informative material on the subject addressed. It is not intended to serve as a replacement for professional medical advice. Any use of the information in this book is at the reader's discretion. The author and publisher specifically disclaim any and all liability arising directly or indirectly from the use or application of any information contained in this book. A healthcare professional should be consulted regarding your specific situation.

Dedication

I dedicate this book to my husband for his love, support and the creative life. To the miracle of finding each other and being on this journey together. And to my amazing daughters, for the joy they bring and for being true to themselves. Thanks, gratitude and love.

Acknowledgements

I am grateful to all who have supported me in writing this book. I have written *The ABCs of Dating* for the men and women whom I have worked with over the many years of my psychotherapy practice and for those I hope to encourage and inspire. I thank all my friends and colleagues who have shared their beautiful and personal stories about their meetings, breakups and quest for love with me. I hope this book will reach others and allow them to enjoy the process of this vital part of their lives and feel a renewal and affirmation about relationships and a sense of hope and courage to move forward with passion and confidence.

I want to thank my mother for her belief in me. Many thanks to Alice, Marion, Bernadette, Ruth, Jeff, Bill, Gabrielle, Olivia and many others for sharing, supportive encouragement and having patience, humor and honesty. I thank my parents for providing a positive blueprint for love and commitment.

To Martin Bergmann, my teacher and mentor, I want to express my appreciation and great admiration for him as an extraordinary human being. Thanks for inspiring the importance of loving connection in my life.

Table of Contents

Dedication iii

Acknowledgements v

Table of Contents vii

Introduction ix

Chapter 1: It Starts With You 1

Chapter 2: Why Do Many People Have Issues with Dating? 15

Chapter 3: Identifying and Overcoming Your Fears 23

Chapter 4: A's: Making a List 31

Chapter 5: Where to Meet People 45

Chapter 6: On the Date 63

Chapter 7: A's: Sex 75

Chapter 8: A's: After the Date 87

Chapter 9: Making the Right Decision for You 95

Chapter 10: The 'B' Phase: Building Blocks of a Relationship . 101

Chapter 11: C's: 'C' is for Commitment 109

Chapter 12: Words to Date (and Live) By 119

Some *ABCs of Dating* Ground Rules 121

Final Thoughts 123

About the Author 125

Introduction

The ABCs of Dating is a book about the quest for love. It takes you through all the ups and downs entailed in the search for it and empowers readers by highlighting some positive and proven strategies for the mental and emotional preparation necessary for true companionship. My aim is to guide you towards being conscious and aware of what to look for in another and encourage you to embrace the often challenging reality of the dating game.

The ABCs of Dating is a unique process which leads from the A Phase of meeting and beginning a relationship, to the B Phase, the middle stages of a relationship and finally to the C Phase, the commitment phase. It's not as straightforward as learning your ABCs, as growth and commitment to growth and learning new strategies is always a process. The purpose is to help you sort through and make sense of the dating process and to simplify it as a component of this quest. However, the book is meant to inspire you to believe that no matter the outcome, you can be happier, more fulfilled with yourself in general, more socially connected and engaged in doing more interesting and vibrant things with your life. Thus the byproducts of the search for love can indeed contribute to possibilities and opportunities for personal growth, happiness and love. This book will be a catalyst for people who believe in love and are willing to try to incorporate this life connection into their lives. Topics include the preparation of the self, overcoming anxieties, the process of how and where to look for like-minded others, the use of social networking, the actual first date and the learning that ensues about the experience, whether positive or negative.

It addresses various stages of *The ABCs of Dating* in a way that makes meaning out of what could be an otherwise chaotic and confusing experience.

As a practicing psychotherapist in New York City, I work intensively with individuals and couples and their issues around intimacy, sexuality and fulfilling relationships. With all the people I've encountered, I realized that a book on *The ABCs of Dating* would serve as a tool for encouraging people to start on the path of attaining the relationship they wish for. In my role as psychotherapist, I have the added advantage of helping people look more clearly at their unconscious motivations and feelings, which may inadvertently thwart them from making sound judgments about dating or that prevents love from unfolding.

Love is not formulaic. It is highly individualized and idiosyncratic and needs to be respected in a unique way. It is a magical feeling and need not be explained away or analyzed when it just "works." Moreover, each person is unique and whilst this dating manual outlines an approach and a system, it allows for the distinct needs of the person who wishes to date. Much of the time, people feel a sense of loss, disappointment and even failure when it comes to dating or relationships. This book addresses the feelings, consciously and unconsciously, that underpin human longings for love and which could determine outcomes for success.

Human beings have a deep yearning to give and receive love, all of which make one more truly human. In this way, too, *The ABCs of Dating* is a new and special approach. Whilst it may provide ideas, strategies and ideas to utilize, it realizes the individuality of each person and their need for a unique and personal outcome.

Whilst not at all judgmental of different reasons to

date, this book primarily will focus on the journey of finding a real and significant love partner, one that embodies both conscious and unconscious longings, one where falling in love for real may indeed happen. *The ABCs of Dating* is a book for all.

Whether looking for same sex or the opposite sex, or whether others are choosing a partner for you and with you, as is the case in some cultures and religious backgrounds, *choosing* with your heart and head is a paramount part of this process. This is your life, your journey and your heart. Even if others decide on who may be right for you based on values and commitment to similar belief systems, love works best when the heart chooses. This means that compatibility on many levels is needed and the commitment has to be there for love to flourish.

This book is a guide that provides a road map for the questions about the dating process. It also provides a solid support system and a catalyst for empowerment in an area which many people experience as daunting.

The ABCs of Dating guides you from understanding what you want and desire, in other words, the motivation for dating and getting out there, to the ultimate goal of your quest. It also covers getting over the inhibitions that restrict you from feeling deserving of love to working through these issues by integrating your head and your heart.

The ABCs of Dating helps people by answering dating questions and helping you to realize that you are not alone in having issues or difficulties in the dating arena. The process also helps you overcome your own fears and anxiety that dating arouses and it helps you resolve past hurts and fears.

The ABCs of Dating can and will inspire you to

continue to enhance your relationships based on key ingredients. This book expresses methods to learn conscious, creative and empowered dating. It will encourage you to be more in control and more aware of, as well as smarter about the dating process. You'll become more mindful in terms of your own choices serving you in seeing your desires met. You'll also be encouraged to avoid the pitfalls along the way which inevitably lead to frustration and disappointments.

The ABCs of Dating will help you to embrace this process, understand the vicissitudes in the process and become more resilient by building a thicker skin and a more optimistic attitude. It also means helping you to develop a healthy relationship with yourself.

The ABCs of Dating is my commitment to you that reading this book and embarking on this journey will allow for the love you long for. Whether making friends, developing a better and more compassionate relationship with yourself is the outcome, or finding the love you have yearned for with another, you have taken a chance with one of life's most human needs.

As Henry Drummond wrote,
"*To love abundantly is to live abundantly, and to love forever is to live forever.*"

Chapter 1: It Starts With You

Let My Heart Be Wise, It Is The God's Best Gift
—Euripides

The ABCs of Dating is my approach to helping you, and many like you, who are struggling in the world of dating to find the right match. Whether old dating habits resulted in looking in the wrong places and thereby did not allow for enough inner growth, it's now time to do things differently and positively. So many dating and relationship books take the approach of how to date from the *outside-in*. They tell you how to get the attention of a potential mate by getting inside their heads. They lure you in with tricks and games that hide behind a fallacy of teaching what the other person wants and thereby giving up your own empowerment. But the book you're holding right now takes a different approach. There are no rules, no regulations and no gimmicks. The book serves to help you to be less confused and go more with your own natural instincts. *The ABCs of Dating* is about asking the self-reflecting questions that prepare you to date successfully and authentically...from the *inside-out*.

I have developed this *ABCs of Dating* approach because it helps to have a mentor to encourage you to embark and move forward in the dating arena. Also, to remind and help you to use your head and your heart in an integrated way and to become more conscious of yourself and the people you may be considering becoming closer to. It starts with you! Once you are ready to take a closer look at yourself and to move into the realm of healthy relationships with yourself and other people, that's when dating becomes enjoyable.

Agenda for Starting Out—Why Are You Dating?

Preparing to date successfully means asking yourself questions and getting in touch with what you want in a mate or life partner. *Why am I dating? Who and what am I looking for? Am I ready to date?* These types of questions need to be asked and reflected upon as part of a continuum of self-understanding and discovery. Embrace them, as exploring each question opens up the possibility of growth.

Do I know the difference between healthy and unhealthy relationships? Are my longings and strivings attainable? Can I open this door to a new beginning? Taking the journey to self-awareness and inner growth means digging deeper; this leads to greater knowledge and self-reflection. Addressing these questions will provide the opportunities for you to have more satisfactory dating experiences and results.

What Are You Looking For?

To start out on the right footing with the dating process, you need to ask yourself: *What are my belief systems about what I can and cannot have? How does this reconcile with what I yearn for? Am I really clear about why and to what end I am embarking on dating?*

Belief systems are ingrained in us beginning at a very early age and the negative ones are the ones that detract and deter us from forming successful, mutually fulfilling relationships. They are often about unresolved issues and fear-based feelings within you. Think of them as the triggers that set you off. Certainly these issues are driven from the inside-out and are really not about the other person. Looking to the other person means that you're placing the focus on them rather on yourself and your needs. Turning conventional theories of having to understand the other person to owning your role in relationships is, in reality, a backwards approach compared to most dating books. Taking that stance essentially means that you are dismissing your own issues, some of which may be repeating patterns for you, and giving short shrift to the accountability necessary to grow. The barometer should be gauging the level of your own happiness, well-being and level of comfort, not over thinking what will make the other person happy, or trying to get inside their heads, predicting their next moves and then acting accordingly.

Ask yourself this: *Am I exhausted from trying to figure out potential significant others, what they want and what they can give me in a relationship?* For many, the answer is a resounding, "Yes!" And since that tactic has not worked, are you willing to consider that it just might not be the right route? While getting to know your potential partner and where they stand in the dating process is important and necessary, it's time to find a new approach that takes your own self more into the equation. Meeting the right kind of quality people is essential. However, you have to focus on yourself first. The idea is for you to succeed in finding a like-minded other who is right for you. This new and healthy approach will allow you to be happier within yourself no matter what the outcome is. Acquiring this inner self confidence often translates into meeting people more naturally and with ease and excitement.

It's time to transform old thinking and poor habits into new belief systems that better serve you. Here's the catch: because anything worthy of success is worthy of your dedication, in order to go through *The ABCs of Dating*, it serves you to be able to look at erroneous belief systems that interfere with honest assessments of yourself. This means bringing them to the surface layer, looking at them truthfully, and facing them in whatever way best helps you to overcome them and replace them with what is more likely your real truth...that you are deserving of and worthy of love and healthy relationships.

Getting Over Inhibitions

In over twenty years of experience as a psychotherapist and dating mentor, one thing is clear: too many people don't feel worthy of love. This belief is the most detrimental of all when it comes to finding a healthy relationship. Seeking affirmation from others (the outside-in approach), is a disservice to you and to any potential partner who is equally worthy of having you in their life.

As *The ABCs of Dating* unfolds for you, let's consider many of the words that are associated with the A stage of dating. As you read through the list below you'll notice that some will conjure up feelings of excitement while others might do the opposite. Pause on each word to notice and observe your feelings when you read them. This is just a simple exercise to get you thinking about words that are related to dating and relationships and how you respond to them emotionally or otherwise. Use the list to notice your reactions because those may be the areas you'll want to work on. It's a method to allow you to go deeper with your feelings about dating and to address issues and feelings that could be overshadowing interest in the dating process. For instance, do the words cause a reaction in you? Do you feel anxious? Does your heart pound with fear? Does your stomach tighten with trepidation? Or do you feel lighter and nod and smile in agreement? Does the word inspire you? Do you feel hopeful? Does it create a sense of excitement in you?

For now, just observe the feelings that emerge within. Use your initial instincts and do not question or second-guess the feeling. Write it down and go with it!

If you'd like, take out a notebook and jot the words down, taking note of which feelings and thoughts come up for you. It's a simple reflection but well worth doing. For example, Anxiety might mean the good butterflies that you feel in your stomach when your date walks through the door. For others, Anxiety might feel akin to fear. Your personal interpretation is what matters.

The A Phase of Dating Key Words:
- Awareness
- Attachment
- Appeal
- Attraction
- Availability
- Anxiety
- Anticipation
- Abandonment
- Ambivalence
- Analysis
- Assessment
- Agenda

Establishing a Bottom Line for Yourself

Dating requires a level of commitment to the process. Frequently, what gets in the way of a clear path to dating is the confusion between what the head says and what the heart wants. Before taking an approach to dating that's new to you, pose the question: *Can I integrate my heart with my head in order to make this work*? This also means being honest with what type of relationship you're looking for. In other words, to be clear, conscious, mindful and present about why and to what end you embark on dating! There are many reasons why you might have noticed and picked up this book. It could be you are looking for some support or guide to assist you on your path. It could be because you are confused by listening to all the rules of what you "should not" do according to other books you are reading. Perhaps it was a gift from someone who wants you to be in a healthy, happy, committed relationship. Knowing the type of relationship you want and the reasons why is imperative to successful dating. To determine the type of relationship you want, consider these questions: *Do you long for kinship or do you want a sexual "hookup"? Do you want a love relationship that includes sexuality, or do you want companionship alone? Do you want to merge with someone to complete yourself or do you feel complete but want to enrich your life and add a deeper connection to it?* Your deepest longings for love and intimacy are in question here and you have an opportunity to address them analytically and openly.

To determine *why* you want a certain type of relationship consider these questions: *Are you dating to increase your social circle and make new friends? Are you dating to try out new restaurants and venues? Are you in a culture where arranged marriages exist? Are you recovering from a loss, a hurt or a divorce? Are you using dating as a way of re-entering life through meeting others? Are you recovering from heartbreak and want to meet others to assuage and normalize this loss?*

As you can see, there are many reasons for people to date, but primary to *The ABCs of Dating*, is to be conscious, clear thinking and honest with yourself and with others in order to make this a meaningful experience and a growth-inducing part of your life. Why not make it FUN at the same time? You can!

Let's assume you feel good about yourself, however, you are lonely for the "real thing" and at times feel vulnerable. But remember, you are human. You do not have to be perfect in order to embark on and participate in this dating arena and find a kindred spirit. Take note that the beginning of the emotional preparedness part of the process can take as long as a few months but it is worth embarking on.

Integrating Your Heart with Your Head

There's a theory that some people lead with their heads while others lead with their hearts. Naturally, a mixture of both makes for a healthier combination than one hundred percent of one or the other. I encourage people to find it within themselves to integrate the two when making choices regarding the possibility of love in their lives. Many agree that there is something magical about meeting, locking eyes and falling in love. However, where love is concerned, there needs to be a combination of that unconscious "spark" of magic and a congruence of goals, values and needs between the two of you.

If we examine the exercise of jotting down your feelings with the key A words, it is likely that these words, such as abandonment, anxiety, and attraction, triggered an emotion within you.

If you go back and look at what you wrote down for the word abandonment, for example, it possibly raised an emotional reaction that reminded you of painful feelings of loss and hurt. This can often mean that you're likely to make decisions with your head to avoid your heart being subjected to such a situation again. The feeling of abandonment could influence you to avoid being open, since many people fear repetition of painful experiences, yet often subconsciously seek them out without realizing it until it's too late. Therefore, coping with your past issues surrounding abandonment could be an example of something you'll have to address in your inside-out approach to dating.

Integrating your head with your heart means using your cognitive, practical thoughts and intelligence in conjunction with your heart's desires. If you use too much of your head, you may be avoiding falling in love. If you use too much of your heart, you may not allow yourself to feel safe enough to surrender your heart and trust another. "Look before you leap" is a good saying to reflect this idea. If you actively observe and recognize when the signs are right, you can let your heart take a risk. It's all about finding balance.

I've noted my definitions below of each of the A words previously listed. See if your reaction to them is different or the same based on how I describe them as they relate to relationships:

- *Awareness* means you're in touch with not only yourself, but those around you. There is little denial and you're able to see things for what they are. The good use of instincts can be applied here too.
- *Attachment* can be both healthy and unhealthy depending on how it's perceived. An attached couple can be in a healthy, loving relationship. There can also be unhealthy, co-dependent attachments. This also has to do with an intimacy quotient. Finding the right level of needed attachment that works well for you and the other is crucial. If you need intimacy and attachment,

find someone who places value on that quality too or there will be a "disconnect" and feelings of dissatisfaction or frustration or longing, which can mean a lack of compatibility.

- *Appeal* often has the connotation of finding someone physically attractive who finds you appealing too. Seeking sexual appeal and physical attraction is not superficial but, in fact, important as often that is the first feeling of a real and palpable connection.
- *Attraction* is the chemistry between two people. It's what makes the heart skip a beat at the sight of your partner. A strong attraction is what usually initiates a relationship. There can be a feeling of "love at first sight," a sense of the "duf, duf duf," beat of the heart! It may not even make sense to you but it is real and visceral and has validity and you should feel good about enjoying it.
- *Availability* isn't limited to someone being physically available to date. It also means being emotionally available, which is often an area where many people have vulnerabilities and sensitivities that keep them from being in a healthy relationship.
- *Anxiety* is normal to a degree; however, in excess it becomes a problem. Butterflies on a first or second date are normal, but when they become overwhelming, there could be a bigger issue that needs to be addressed.
- *Anticipation* is the state of excitement that you feel when you know you're going to see and be with your date, who you hope to get to know better. It's the mixture between anxiety and excitement that lets you know that the

anticipation feels special to you. You are probably harboring hopes of you two liking each other and a possible relationship ensuing.

- *Abandonment* is often an "issue" that many people have due to a variety of reasons, including the experience of people leaving them emotionally. These thoughts and feelings can be from lack of warmth, love or attunement or physically through absences like death, divorce, loss etc. It starts in childhood and commonly carries over to adulthood if not dealt with and understood on a deep and personal level. It can also interfere with moving forward with an intrepid stance and open mind and heart.
- *Ambivalence* is the confusion often felt about all the myriad feelings you may have. It may be about the person you are seeing and underlying conflicts within yourself about a variety of generated feelings. These feelings can be centered on the reality versus the fantasy of who this person is and the anxiety in sorting this out and getting to know them. Ambivalence can mean that you're hesitant about relationships in general and undecided as to your real longings. It can also reflect an unwillingness or inability within yourself to be certain of your own truths. In *The ABCs of Dating*, you are encouraged to be on good terms with yourself and trust your choices and listen to your unconscious.
- *Analysis* of yourself and the other person you are meeting and what transpires during your time together is an important part of the dating process. This examination is especially necessary after the date but oftentimes before. Sometimes

having an objective, neutral voice outside of your own self can help lead you forward and help you to know yourself and interpret the truth of a situation more quickly. In dating, this is important as you are trying not to get caught up in sheer fantasy but to live in reality and hope that you can blend magic with practicality. But be careful who you do talk to and be sure that they have your best interests at heart. Friends can be biased; family can tell you that you are always longing for something ephemeral or want you to connect even if you are sharing what is amiss with them.

- *Assessment* (based on your preparation of what you would ideally need) is a conclusion of needs and desires as well as what you need to focus on in order to achieve them.
- *Agenda* is what everyone has, whether it's hidden or out in the open. It's a plan, a wish, a desire that, when in a relationship, often involves a potential partner. There is nothing wrong with having an agenda. The key is having an agenda that you feel good about; one that is part of your narrative and that you can share with another. And having an agenda means you can be respectful of their agenda too and assess whether there is a mutuality of interest in moving forward together.

As part of the process of integrating your heart with your head, there are some additional questions you should be asking yourself in this A Phase.

Can I review my previous dating experiences so they do not sabotage the present ones?

If you answer "yes" to this, then it shows that you're taking steps toward using your head to heal your emotional wounds. Take the time to review your previous dating experiences and see what the common denominators are. *What did you put forth in the relationships and what were you willing to compromise that contributed to unsuccessful relationships?* Work through these experiences and take note of ways you can avoid them in the future. People have a way of making the same mistakes over and over. *The ABCs of Dating*, and this part of the book, can help stop this repetition from continuing by encouraging you to be clear and honest with yourself.

The Merriam-Webster Dictionary describes posture as a *"state or condition at a given time especially with respect to capability in particular circumstances."* Readjusting your posture will require you to be aware of past trends. When you do this, you can adjust your own behavior as you move forward with greater clarity. It's wise not to bring your past hurts and mistakes into the next relationship or to carry all your baggage with you. Were you too active, not letting things unfold or too passive and not asking enough questions? If you're ready to take ownership of your dating experiences, you'll do well through the A Phase of dating. And you will enjoy it so much more!

Here are some important questions to ask yourself to help you to begin, to reflect, to understand and to provide you with a more clear focus on that process:

- *Am I inadvertently getting in my own way?* Take pause to think about whether you're sabotaging yourself no matter what happened in the past. Stay involved in the process moment by moment.
- *Am I open to learning about myself on a deeper level?*

- *Am I willing to address, understand and change my own behaviors that contributed to the downfall of past relationships?*
- *Am I looking at my choices? Or am I locked into one idea of what I want in another person without being open to other ideas?*
- *Am I over the hurt and disappointment from the past if things did not go my way? Or do I still need to do some work on myself about this?*
- *Do I trust that I will keep going and will not let fear or hurt stop me?*
- *Do I understand the meaning of a "healthy interdependency" or am I either overtly dependent or too independent and even distant?* Note: This could translate into either trying to make anything work because of intense dependency needs and longings or it could result in pushing people away because of fears of becoming too close, overly enmeshed or engulfed.
- *Am I experiencing fear of abandonment and rejection so much that it is clouding the entire process?* Do not let these feelings make you fearful so that you lose sight of what is truly happening when meeting people. It's important to have an open heart and be excited about new possibilities.
- *Are feelings such as abandonment and rejection impacting the ability to be clear and open, making you lose sight of the goals and dreams you wanted?*

When you can address your deepest fears and live with them, rather than letting them overtake you, it is even more possible to go for the best for yourself!

Chapter Summary:

The A of *The ABCs of Dating* is a real process of self-reflection helping you to understand if you've been looking at dating with a clear head and an open heart. It empowers you to take the inside-out approach to dating and to dial down the influences of the outside. It is the beginning of the process and will help you to know you are not alone in struggling with many of the issues and fears involved with dating.

The idea is to have your eyes and heart open and your mind in a questioning, curious and positive learning stance. This is a great place to start!

Chapter 2: Why Do Many People Have Issues with Dating?

Gravitation is not responsible for people falling in love.
—Albert Einstein

Being Honest With Yourself

One of the biggest hurdles in the A Phase is being honest enough in your self-evaluations. With this honesty, you can make the progress needed to find the match you deserve and one who deserves you. It's truly exciting to think about meeting that special person: what they'll be like, how you'll be together and all the good feelings that go with meeting the right person. To get there takes hard work and being honest enough with yourself and your past in order to wholeheartedly embrace the process. All aspects of the process should be worth the effort of achieving your goals. And no matter what, you cannot lose if you are valuing yourself and you are trying. Whether you utilize talk therapy, programs, books, or groups, keeping yourself tuned into your past and using your inner guidance is key to breaking down walls and ridding yourself of old habits. This is all necessary to create a new present and future that you long for.

It's all part of the inside-out approach to dating; you have to get yourself ready to meet your "just-right" person for you! At the same time, they have to be ready to meet you, so hopefully they are doing the same work you are in one form or another. The more people dig in and make the self-exploratory efforts that are needed to be in a healthy relationship, the more healthy relationships will evolve as a result.

There is magic! This is not a science or even an art

form, just a very human part of life relating to a deep human longing for connection and for love.

An unknown author said, "*Once you have learned to love, you have learned to live.*" Keep going and the motivation will become clearer as this excellent part of the journey of your life unfolds.

Anxiety Provoking

I know that doing this alone can feel challenging and daunting. That's why people are drawn into getting help with these kinds of relationship longings and why I deal with these themes frequently. *The ABCs of Dating* helps you work through and understand in an enlightened fashion the barriers, fears, stereotypes and projections that need to be looked at so you can emerge and break through to personal fulfillment. A person undertaking this task alone may go round and round and not be able to get to a new place on their own.

Dating Isn't Always Fun

The idea that *dating isn't always fun* really takes shape with most people after they've had enough dates that did not yield positive returns. This kind of track record can leave people feeling hopeless or disappointed in all the longings it can evoke. Trust that these experiences will diminish as you go through the process of clearing out old emotions that are holding you back.

Sometimes meeting people more mindfully and with intention can feel like work. But it doesn't have to feel that way if you know what you want and choose quality ways to meet people. If you consider taking care of yourself and recognize the possibility of love as a great outcome, then this will help you to overcome your antipathy about this process. Learning about oneself on a deeper level can sometimes be painful. Disappointments are difficult to process and it can be hard to keep going. But you can put trust that your own intelligence and the strategies provided in *The ABCs of Dating* will help you to feel stronger and even enthusiastic about dating. Walt Whitman wrote *"Do anything, but let it produce joy."* Try to remember this through all the stages of dating.

Rather than take on the "work" of dating, many people rely on the romantic fantasy of meeting their mate in an organic or spontaneous way, for instance, in a movie line, at the supermarket or browsing in a bookstore. The idea of meeting someone this way usually feels exciting as the unexpected encounter can result in a jolt of physical and tangible attraction.

While chance encounters can bring the feeling of Hollywood magic to your life, they don't make you exempt from assessing whether you are emotionally ready and truly available to meet someone. A new relationship is not always the cure for Friday nights alone on the couch with your cat and the Hallmark Channel. It's not the solution for dealing with an insistent family member who hounds you about when you're going to find someone. The only truly successful path to take is the one you give yourself by attempting to make new choices and by coming to terms with feelings of loneliness, abandonment, cynicism and even distaste for the process of dating.

The idea of a serendipitous and chance encounter is compelling in that it often rids the nerves of a first date. Say, for example, you meet someone in a park while taking a walk and you end up sitting and talking with them for hours. It happens so naturally that it feels like fate. This can well be a wonderful beginning.

Alternatively, many people meet through *proactive*

methods, such as a blind date or online dating. There's no doubt that first dates can be wonderful! Yet, no matter how the date came about, the idea of meeting someone at a set time in a set place comes with added pressures that a chance encounter, by nature, simply doesn't have. If you've experienced both, you already know that they each have their own advantages and different levels of excitement. Those few minutes of waiting for someone in the coffee shop can feel like a mix of excitement and anxiety. That's not something you get with a chance encounter that sweeps in unexpectedly! The beauty of *The ABCs of Dating* is that it can open you up to yourself and your feelings. It can help you to feel that life touches you more and that you are generally more social, happier and more open with each date you go on.

When your approach to dating changes, so do the results, and that's what my goal is...to help you change your attitude and become more empowered and knowledgeable. As your subjective inner world shifts about dating and your part in it, you will find that you can have more fulfilling dates and relationships.

If you really struggle with the idea of dating, I recommend that you see a psychotherapist who specializes in dating and relationships to interpret your dating goals. I do this work with people and this process is helpful and empowering. Proper guidance in the form of outside help can translate to the inside work getting done, thereby making dating less anxiety-provoking and more enjoyable for you.

Red Flags

A "Red Flag" is a triggered inner recognition device that helps you become aware of what could potentially be a problem or an issue. Red flags are sometimes observations of negative qualities and signs of behavior or even pathology in people you would want to avoid at all costs. Or they may be indicators that there is potential for you to keep going, but you need to ask more questions and learn more about this person.

No matter how you meet someone, whether it's through a friend, online dating, or in line at the grocery store, at least you're out there meeting people and giving dating a try. Yet being aware of any "red flags" for both you and your potential mate is a must.

Staying in tune with red flags and how big of a flag they are takes practice and awareness. As you become more experienced in dating and in knowing your own needs, they will stand out bigger and brighter and you will learn to avoid potential pitfalls, allowing you to move on and find your true partner. We will go into more detail about red flags throughout the book, including the internet dating section.

If You've Been Hurt

Being hurt in relationships is something we all experience. It's part of our growth and development and contributes to how we move forward or don't move forward in other relationships. Part of being hurt is recovering and broken hearts are no different. The time and method it takes to heal will be different with each person and each scenario but it's a process that you should go through in order to recover from those past hurts.

If you haven't recovered and you've met someone new you may assume you're ready for a new relationship. We sometimes, however, get tripped up based on the longing and need for love, so we may misjudge the reality of the situation and how it might unfold. If you can take on the emotional healing work needed to move forward and be objective and honest with yourself ahead of time, you'll realize the truth of your past situations and how continuing to have them as beliefs will only be a disservice to future relationships. Commit to yourself first so that you can become the kind of person you want to be when you start dating. Being more aware of emotional blocks, more free of previously painful relationships, you will naturally attract like-minded and openhearted people into your life. At that point, the past hurts will reside where they belong: in the past. You can then dedicate yourself to a new and different future and to being open to happiness in the present. This is the emotional preparedness part of the journey with all the "working through" you may need to undertake along with continued self-reflection. This all helps in allowing and providing a commitment to the new beginnings you are excited about! To quote Walt Whitman here again, *"Keep your face always toward the sunshine—and shadows will fall behind you."*

Chapter Summary:

Everyone experiences hurt from relationships that didn't work out in the past. In order to move forward you need to get beyond these hurts and release the inhibitions of what you think you cannot have or are not deserving of.

Dating does take time and reflection so that you can become the more open and less fearful person you want to be when you enter the dating world. Many people who have not gone into it with clarity and self-reflection end up with residual issues that can create repetition of fears that can block emotional happiness. Doing the work ahead of time will allow you to start the process with a healthy approach rather than risking repeating old patterns. It will help you to avoid repeating those painful feelings of hurt and abandonment and regret. This is about learning and beginning again positively with self-reflection and responsibility for your choices.

Preparing yourself for a healthy relationship frequently means going outside yourself in order to go inside. Whether it's through therapy, books or programs, finding the right help to unclutter the old mental models that weren't working for you is important to your continued growth. The fact that you're reading this now is strong validation that you are on the right track!

Chapter 3: Identifying and Overcoming Your Fears

Love does not consist of gazing at each other, but in looking together in the same direction.
—*Antoine De-Saint-Exupery*

Overcoming Inner Fear

In this initial A Phase of *The ABCs of Dating*, coping with and overcoming fears is all a part of your journey.

"Fear" is often an umbrella term for many other underlying emotions. In this chapter we'll address some feelings that can create fears around intimacy, such as abandonment, engulfment, disappointment and lack of trust. These are in fact fears that influence your dating successes. They may not all apply to you but it is worth working through the ones that do as this will put you on the right path toward finding your mate.

The importance of love is uniquely human. Starting from birth humans need love in order to survive. Our connection with parents and early caregivers is vital to our overall health and functioning. The longing for love remains a part of the human experience. There is an innate need not only to be loved but *to* love. To feel alive, connected to a life force and others in a positive way is vital to our overall health. To experience the unknown mystery of the journey of meeting another that sparks a familiar and special feeling for many is the essence of life that most people yearn for.

My purpose here is to encourage you to open up to embracing that human need for connection and love in its various forms. In order to embrace this, we also need to look at where our fears were developed so that we can overcome them and tap back into that love that is innately within us. Whilst one's heart needs to feel moved, one's thoughts are another important part of *The ABCs of Dating*. Embracing the connection love brings will enrich the process and allow for even greater opportunities for successful dating and the fulfillment of the dream for a loving relationship.

Fears can cause great distress. They have the ability to create emotional turmoil that can contribute towards making you feel emotionally paralyzed. Try to understand your fears and deal with them directly so that you can move past them, break old patterns and confidently move on. One of the biggest successes you can achieve is to attempt to overcome your inner fears regarding dating. You want to have richer dating experiences that are more positive and put you into the best posture to achieve an outcome that your heart desires.

Fearful

The state of being fearful frequently begins in childhood. Fear of the dark, fear of loud noises, fear of being alone, fear of parental abandonment, fear of judgment and fear of deprivation are just a few that you could probably come up with from your own life experiences. How deeply embedded these fears were allowed to become had a lot to do with your home life and upbringing and whether or not there was help and support from family, friends, teachers, peers and role models.

This book is meant to address people of all walks of life. Even people with trauma can overcome their issues with the right kind of help. The good news is that people are capable of growth to go beyond past hurts. You are deserving of and can be a part of a healthy, vibrant relationship in the present. I've seen it happen many, many times even with those who are coming from difficult circumstances. The world is truly full of promise and you are capable of living and having it.

Abandonment

Abandonment is a common fear. In varying degrees, we have all felt the feeling of abandonment at one point or another. Once again, it's a fear that begins in childhood and carries forward into adulthood. Feeling abandoned can be devastating to people's sense of self and cohesion and can be difficult to deal with. However, you can do so by exploring situations in your past where these feelings occurred and by realizing that these feelings need not be repeated by making better choices in the present.

When you bring abandonment issues into relationships, the consequences can include feeling anxious, nervous and needy. It can result in clingy and unempowered behavior. Your best intention would be to realize that these feelings are about old, unresolved issues of abandonment. *Is your date whom you barely know kicking up these feelings in you? If so, why? Is this about the present or about the past? Are these feelings being projected by you onto your partner or are they being activated by your partner's behavior?* Open your eyes to these kinds of feelings and reactions and you will find that it helps you tolerate and overcome deep-seated fears about dating and falling in love.

One of the best ways to resolve past abandonment issues is to look back at the period in your life when those feelings first started. Identifying an event or trauma, and looking at it with a new perspective and with the eyes of an adult, rather than a child, will help to clarify what you felt and what created these issues. You are about growth and new resolutions!

Try this Exercise: Create a timeline of life events
- *When have you felt abandoned in your life?*
- *Have you truly overcome abandonment issues?*
- *If so, how long did it take you to rebound?*
- *If not, how might you go about resolving them?*
- *Are you particularly vulnerable and sensitive to feeling abandoned?*
- *Was it one powerful event such as a life trauma that created this or was it an ongoing feeling of, for instance, not feeling loved?*

Examining these past situations and how they may be impacting your current relationships is not always clear. It's important to do the work now before you start dating. It can provide insight as well as a sense of compassion for yourself as you traverse this new terrain.

It's important that you look forward to dating, despite all your fears and concerns. Do not feel isolated or alone and enlist help if you find you need it. You owe it to yourself to sort out in your mind what behaviors in the actual date make you nervous or whether your own insecurities are kicking up. If your date is reliable and consistent, then do not allow your fears to overtake you!

Engulfment

Engulfment is being overwhelmed by the needs of another. It encompasses the threat of losing your sense of self for another and the idea that being with them may take you from your own pursuits. This may make you fearful of dating and can be a strong impediment to being in a committed relationship. It means you experience a feeling of losing your own space, a feeling that another's needs dominate, where taking time for yourself may feel compromised.

Fear not! No one can "take you over" unless you give them this yourself. It is up to you to set boundaries and limits and then ascertain whether your need for intimacy mirrors your partner's or whether you are inherently not in sync. Some people are highly interpersonal and love to be in a state of hyper-connectedness in ways that can come with being in a very close relationship. Others may be the more detached, "ice climbing in Alaska" kind of person who does not require or demand such day-to-day closeness and who likes the balance of long periods of time alone yet may want a deep and close relationship, too.

It is your job to clearly understand your own needs so that you can find someone *you* feel compatible with. That way you will not feel engulfed, nor will you feel abandoned. In other words, if you are a person to whom regular contact is important, find someone similar in this area, or you will feel frustrated and could interpret their indifference to be personal.

Disappointment

It should be becoming clear by now that many of the issues raised in this chapter are based on feelings that began early on in life and have continued into adulthood. Do not let them play out in your current life. The good news is that as an adult, you have an opportunity to look at your current feelings objectively and with curiosity and compassion. This allows growth from past experiences. You are trying to achieve a greater sense of control and awareness of your feelings and their influence in the present. The results can allow for a change in outlook, choices and even perceptions and for potentially more fulfilling dating and love experiences.

Disappointment is an emotion that we feel on a small to large scale. Feelings of disappointment can be evoked from things that we enjoy and that give us pleasure. For example, a restaurant being out of your favorite dessert or your favorite sports team losing a game, or a close friend canceling a long awaited meeting, are examples of disappointments on a small scale. Personal disappointments on a larger scale might be not getting a job you wanted, or a close friend moving away, or the end of a long-term relationship. These are examples of important feelings that can create feelings of hurt, loss and disappointment that need understanding through addressing them.

Much like fear or abandonment, disappointment can present itself in various shapes and forms. It's the *level* of disappointment that you allow yourself to get caught up in that determines your peace and happiness. As it relates to dating, disappointment can stem from being stood up on a first date to the relationship not progressing in the way you may have hoped for. Ultimately, all disappointments have to do with the expectations that form in your mind; longings, hopes and desires easily imagined can sometimes fall short of reality.

Disappointment is part of the process of engaging with others. Seeing it for what it is and then letting it go is what's needed to move forward. When you process and release the small disappointments quickly, you're one step closer to being less affected by things you cannot change and being less fragile in terms of your feelings.

Lack of Trust

Trust is often the number one quality desired in a relationship. We know that without building trust, a relationship cannot truly develop and that without any or enough trust, a relationship on shaky grounds cannot continue to unfold and grow in a healthy way.

In *The ABCs of Dating*, establishing and building trust is an important part of figuring out whether or not you should proceed in a relationship with a given person. You need the time and a variety of experiences to know someone well enough to ascertain whether trust is mutually there. It's smart not to trust someone too quickly from the start, but rather take the time to get to know them. One of the ways in which trust builds is through spoken words. Actions are another way we learn about the trustworthiness of our partner. Together, words and actions act as the building blocks that create the foundation of a relationship. Just like a building, if those words and actions are weak, the foundation will crumble. Alternatively, if they are strong, then the foundation will survive and trust can ensue.

For some who have had trust broken over the years, it may take even more time to truly know you have found someone trustworthy. Broken promises and bad relationships in the past may have contributed to a lack of trust that has carried over to relationships throughout our lives. Therefore, it's only natural that we would want to trust the person we are getting to know before we surrender our hearts and our bodies.

It's not helpful when you bring past hurts into current situations. Couples should earn one another's trust. At the same time, if you can think back to times in your life when someone you trusted let you down, and explore and analyze those situations for what they were, including your own role in them, you'll be doing the inner work that will help you heal.

Trust provides the emotional safety necessary for really healthy relationships to continue to grow and to unfold positively. Emotional safety creates a chance to communicate honestly and with greater ease and fewer fears of rejection or hurt emerging. We want people to trust us as much as we want to trust them. When you find a person whom you can develop a mutual trust with, you are well on your way to a successful relationship.

Remember that trusting someone means being able to do so in all areas of your relationship; from promises made to feeling safe with them personally and sexually. As time goes by, you'll each be given many opportunities, big and small, to continue to build upon trust. Being faithful and honest is an important way to keep the momentum going, so make every effort to portray trustworthiness as you would want from your partner as well.

Chapter Summary:

Fear is a natural feeling that we all experience from past relationship issues. It can take many forms that ultimately inhibit and block current happiness. While it is common in everyone, it is also an emotion that must be worked through in order to be open to the relationship you really want and all future potential.

Giving and receiving trust, getting over abandonment issues, not fearing engulfment and coping with disappointments are all aspects of doing inner work that can lead to an emotionally healthy life and more fulfilling relationships.

Chapter 4: A's: Making a List

"Love looks not with the eyes, but with the mind, And therefore is winged Cupid painted blind."
—William Shakespeare

Your A List

One tool I highly recommend in *The ABCs of Dating* is making a list of desirable qualities in a partner. This task allows you to prepare yourself for meeting the right person. And actually writing this list down is a vital part of the A Phase.

Sit down and write out your list of what you need in a relationship. You will refer to and add to it as you go along, but making your "A List" is a real opportunity to work on yourself, to make conscious choices, and to also access your subconscious longings. It's a tool of longing and practicality that you can refer to and update as you learn more about yourself and others.

Making a list will help you get beyond the inhibitions around what you think you cannot have or are not deserving of when it comes to love and a relationship. Putting your ideals to paper will help integrate your heart and your longings and make the whole dating experience more fruitful and manageable when you adhere to your list or adjust it accordingly.

To best embrace this process, sit in a quiet place and give yourself the time and space to really think about what to put down. Not because it will be etched in stone, but because doing so allows you to reflect on what hasn't worked in the past and what qualities you want in a partner going forward.

The first question people often ask is: *What should be on my list?* Your list should consist of the *essential* and *desirable* qualities you feel you need in a life partner and a relationship. These can be new ideas that occur to you as you start writing or they can be ideas that you've known all along are vital for you to have in another person and a relationship. This means that your list should consist of traits, qualities and values that you have thought long and hard about as well as new ideas that develop throughout the dating process. With your list, you will become closer to achieving the relationships you want by clarifying your intentions as they were initially set out when you started this process.

The List Itself

When you sit down to write your list, don't edit yourself. Just write out everything that comes to mind regarding what you need and want as well as your values and goals. Don't worry about what anyone else would think or say about what you are writing because this exercise and list are for you and you alone.

I recommend starting with your IDEAL mate. For example, consider what you long and hope for and start writing down your ideas. Although it's often the physical attraction that creates a spark, having the same values and future goals are critical. In healthy relationships, ultimately there needs to be a blend of sexuality and love under one umbrella. So, while it's okay to list, "tall, dark and handsome," or "supermodel figure," you also do yourself a great favor by having an open mind and by being flexible.

The idea of being flexible and even compromising on your list is that *you* are the one who decides where you're able and willing to be flexible when you meet someone who doesn't match your list exactly. Being open to something that may not be the most conventional relationship can be fun and a game-changer in the right circumstance. If someone lives in a different state but still lives close enough for frequent visits and has fantastic potential for you, are you willing to compromise and travel a bit further to see each other? What other areas are you able to look at and possibly adjust your perspectives? What adjustments can make you feel as though you're still making great choices?

Your list might include some of these ideals: intelligence, fidelity, supportiveness, emotional stability, sense of humor, age range, looks that appeal to you, etc.

Don't feel like you have to focus on creating the perfect list. Just getting it all down on paper is perfect. Therefore, there's no need to get caught up in any anxiety around listing what's right or completing your list. Keep in mind that this list can and frequently does change as you go through the process of *The ABCs of Dating*. Later, once you've been out dating and experiencing different situations, your list can always be adjusted.

Here Are Some Additional Tips and Guidance:
- Think of making your list as though you're making a stew. Only put in it what you absolutely HAVE to have in order to make it delicious. What are the primary ingredients? Then think about other lesser ingredients that are desirable but not entirely necessary. What might add flavor but may not be absolutely necessary?
- Then, add some extras that may surprise you and would be desirable. What gives substance and would be a great surprise but not essential to you?

For instance, your ideal partner may be a good cook or more essentially, enjoy sharing cooking with you. Do they need to play a musical instrument to make it onto the "ideal" list or is it enough that they support your interest and enjoyment in music?
- If you think about what you would NOT want in a mate, turn it around and list the ideal that you would like.
- Remember, you cannot ask for what you yourself cannot give in return. In other words, when you read your list, do the qualities also apply to you? This means that what you expect, you can give back, creating a mutually appreciative relationship. For example, are you honest and trustworthy in a relationship? Do you have integrity, a stable career, or anything else that you might list?

With this idea in mind, rewrite or add qualities to your list and consider what you would like to receive in return. Examples would be:

- Someone I find attractive who finds me attractive too.
- Someone capable of monogamy who desires my monogamy in return.
- Someone who longs to have a family and wants one with me.
- Someone who does not mind that I have a family from a previous relationship.
- Someone who values intelligence and the way you see things.
- Someone who is supportive of my social life and

enjoys the fact that I have many friends and introduces me to their friends too.
- Someone who has many interests and shares them as I share mine.
- Someone who has a similar need for sex and intimacy, making us sexually and emotionally compatible.
- Someone who values financial responsibility and appreciates that I have this need as well.

Depending on your age group, what you write down can make a big difference in the types of characteristics you add to your list. If you are younger, you may feel more entitled to list someone who doesn't have children. If you are middle aged or older, it may be unrealistic to expect to meet people who do not have children or an ex-spouse or a reason for not having been in a serious relationship. There are many permutations in these scenarios.

The important thing is to be true to yourself and list what really counts for your current lifestyle needs and goals and to be aware of how you too would like to be received. Being realistic in terms of age, culture, background and in matters of what your heart longs for, is what you are thinking about whilst creating your list.

In other cases, cultural and religious similarities may impact your list. Consider all aspects of your lifestyle, obligations to family and culture and anything else that impacts a relationship and then list them!

Refinding

The unconscious process of finding and refinding significant others based on early parenting and role models is a common one. One of Freud's most powerful theories is the concept of refinding. Refinding means that you find someone similar to your loved ones in your past; your parents, grandparents, siblings and caregivers, which creates a blueprint of what one looks for in the present. You may consciously want to think of the qualities of these people and find people in the present who remind you of them, especially if they were people who were positive influences in your life.

Sometimes when people create their list, they subconsciously use the "refinding" way. When writing your list, take into consideration all of the positive qualities your caregivers and families contributed to your upbringing in order to identify the ones that would work for you in the present.

If you consciously think of these people and some of their positive qualities to add to your list, you'll help to keep your "refinding" experience a positive one. Alternatively, if your parent was an alcoholic, you may find the person you are drawn to is familiar in this regard. It would be beneficial for you to make the effort not to repeat familiar negative habits and traits. On the other hand, if you loved your parents' nurturing ways, you may want to find someone who nurtures you whilst realizing that this person is similar but different from your parents. Another example would be if your parent was overly gratifying and so idealized by you, it could detract from you in the present from finding someone as you may be overly attached to that parent and not be truly open to letting someone else in. Also, they should be similar but not so similar as to thwart the ability to be sexual, and they should not be so different as to feel too different to relate to. There is a magical interweaving of both conscious and subconscious longings and the need for day to day compatibility and value systems that make relationships work.

Another example may be if you were exposed to infidelity in your childhood and it created related insecurities for you. In your love relationships you may have subconsciously chosen to experience this without realizing it. Maybe former partners were incapable of fidelity or maybe you too had issues with it. So now that you are taking a new approach, it's important to find someone who values and believes in fidelity, so this experience from your childhood will not repeated. This is an example of using conscious awareness to only draw in and allow what (and who) works for you now. But remember, you cannot just take these qualities for granted or assume that people have them. You need to talk, to share, to communicate and get to know people before you can make such a determination. You may be disappointed that they differ vastly from you in some important areas yet there still may be areas of great overlap. By dealing with the reality of learning who they are, you are choosing for yourself if they are right for you. Mutual compatibility is what you are going for. This is a time for honest assessments and really listening to the voice inside your head.

All of these aspects are worth considering before or while you are making your list. Dating does take energy and enthusiasm. Writing down your list is your first attempt at going for the gold! You are playing, exploring and enjoying the idea and meaning of a great partnership in its IDEAL form for you. There is only success in this approach!

Next Steps

Once you start applying *The ABCs of Dating* as you actively date, you will likely feel inclined to edit or adjust your list. That happens frequently and is, in fact, a great sign that the process is working. You will find yourself seeing things in a whole new light and a clearer one at that. You may find yourself removing some of the qualities that were previously listed or adding new ones that you hadn't fully considered. For example, it is okay to be specific, such as listing that you want someone who lives in the same city, but does he or she really need to live within a ten block radius? By becoming less rigid, you could likely remove this from your list after dating enough people. However, if you have ruled out a long distance relationship (i.e. you live in another state or several hours away) because of its unique complications, then it's okay to stick with that.

In this same regard, no matter your culture, it is important to think clearly about your bottom line: the kind of qualities you consciously want in a relationship and partner. Note that this still applies even in cases where you have parents arranging your marriage, or are working with a matchmaker, or come from a background where it's expected for you to find a partner within your group! Others may do the legwork for you but, ultimately, your list still needs to exist since everyone is unique. And together you have to choose one another on a deeper level, besides the overt and similar qualities you have set down in your list.

As such, you may find it easier to have two lists. For example:
- An *Essentials List:* Qualities you really want in an ideal relationship.
- A *Desired List:* I would like this, but don't absolutely require it.

The first list outlines the ideals of the type of relationship you want; whereas the second includes more qualities you might like someone to have but which are not essential. Remember to be thorough as you do this exercise as it will ground you and help you when you are finally out there dating "in the field." You'll have your list to refer to in your psyche and it will help you to stay on track when learning about who this person is and whether or not they are good for you.

Remember, the right person, who can meet your needs as you can meet his or hers in return, is out there for you. Maintain your positive attitude about both your list and your experiences. Many people find themselves feeling very creative, excited and alive when they start dating with this process. You may find yourself on a date and thinking about adding a certain quality you had forgotten about. You may find yourself waking in the early hours of the morning and adding to your list.

It's all fun and good as you open up again to your longings and your needs. You will feel more secure and confident in going out there into the world and seeing and discovering more people and who they really are in relation to what you're looking for in a partner.

Here are some list ideas to ponder:
- Qualities that you feel you need in a life partner that resonate deeply within you.
- Lifestyle ideals that you know would match your own.
- The role of physical compatibility and shared interests.

Examples of Essential Qualities:
This list below is a great example of things that could be on your Essentials list:
- Physically Healthy
- Gainfully Employed
- Single
- Similar Interests
- Non-substance Abuser
- Emotionally Stable
- Good Values
- Strong Family Relations
- Integrity
- Honest
- Makes and Follows Through with Commitments
- Adventurous
- Fun Loving
- Responsible
- Sense of Humor
- Intelligence
- Mature
- Emotionally Healthy
- Speaks Portuguese

Examples of Desired Aspects:

I've seen many great "*Would be Great*" lists. Here are some fun things I've seen on them:
- Washboard Abs
- Heir to a Chocolate Fortune
- Never Married
- Drives a Nice Car
- Tall, Dark and Handsome
- Hirsute
- Can fly a kite
- Is bald
- Knows how to choose a French wine

Ideally, the items on your *Essentials* list are qualities you can give back to your partner. Naturally, your *Desired* list brings different ideals; ones that are not all-important. Some qualities do not need to be ones you possess in return. It may be fine for you to find a triathlete whilst you would rather be on the sidelines cheering them on. People are different and luckily, you can find uniqueness in every person. Certain people may enrich your life through new experiences and interests. It's all what works for two individual adults and part of the fun of finding compatibilities.

Remember, this process is not meant to become a clinical method devoid of love, creative longing or having a great time. We will never discount basic chemistry or attraction. That's the "magic" that people feel when falling in love! The lists are meant to flexible and to inspire and empower. This is your chance to actively set the best direction for what you need, what you want and who you are.

The key here is to *actively* create the lists. Besides making the lists you can utilize methods like role models and vision boards.

Role models of great couples

Think about couples you know and admire and utilize the attributes they have as role models in your search for love. If you find yourself experiencing envy about their relationship, utilize this feeling in your own interests. This way, your envy can become a positive catalyst for your being more able to articulate desirable qualities and strive to attain them.

Vision Boards

For some people, especially the visual people amongst us, making a vision board is a fun addition to writing a list. If you aren't familiar with the concept of a vision board, think of it as a collage of images, not unlike one you would create on Pinterest. The culmination of images represents the kind of love life you want.

Combining a list with a vision board could be an approach that brings more insight for you. If your list says you want someone who enjoys taking walks in the park, you can then find an image (either in a magazine or online,) of a couple walking in a park and add that to your vision board. If your desire is to find someone who can cook with you, look for an image of a couple cooking in the kitchen.

The key to vision boards is the fun and emotional energy you put into creating them.

Once your vision board is made, keep it in sight where you can see it daily and remind yourself of the life you want to see come to fruition. Just like your list, you can also add new pictures to your vision board as you go through your dating process. Looking at all of the images can be like watching a movie in your mind of the life you want to have. Make an evening of it and keep it lively and enjoyable. This is all part of dating, and yes, it can be fun.

Chapter Summary:

Making your Essentials and Desired Lists will help you get beyond the inhibitions of what you think you cannot have or are not deserving of. Making a list will help integrate your heart and your longings with a lot of common sense so as to make the whole dating experience more clear, creative and useful. Dating does take energy and enthusiasm. Do not allow your trepidation of dating to put you in the position of feeling overly vulnerable, hurt and fearful. Maintain faith in yourself.

By achieving clarity through the A stage, you will be more likely to steer clear of people who would not resonate with you or be a healthy match. By creating your lists, you are much more likely to have greater self-awareness. You can avoid inappropriate partners who you would be poorly matched with. By being clear about what you want and need, you will avoid those people as potential partners as they won't align with your list of what is essential for your emotional wellbeing.

Doing the work in the A stage of dating with a compassionate approach will help to foster and build positive feelings about being entitled to go for and find the person who has the kind of qualities that would make you happy.

Chapter 5: Where to Meet People

Whoso loves, believes the impossible
—Elizabeth Barret Browning

Now that you have a good understanding of what kind of person you're looking for, you have to go out and make yourself available to finding them. This comes more naturally to more outgoing people but if you pick venues that make you feel comfortable, you'll be more at ease. The ideas below are suggestions for places to start.

Serendipity vs. Intentional Meetings

Chance encounters are the serendipitous ones that can actually happen in many ways. Social events, speed dating, online dating and meet-up groups are more formal ways. Other spontaneous ways are when you meet someone when you're out and about, in line at the bookstore or grocery shopping or at the beach.

When you meet under these circumstances and it leads to a first date, excitement and even a bit of that intoxicating anxiety take over. By the time you meet them at the coffee shop or café or wherever you agree on, you've told your closest friends that you've met an amazing person. You've bought a new dress or a shirt to wear and you've probably talked on the phone with him or her a few times before the date, something I definitely recommend.

Sound familiar? It's okay to be excited about meeting someone new. But remember that the reality of who they are unfolds in the days, weeks and months to come. This is the time needed to spend with them so that you can see them in many settings and different moods in order to get a clearer sense of whether you can and should proceed into a more committed relationship. Despite that initial, powerful connection, the reality is that you don't know them yet. That also means you don't know if they're ready for the kind of relationship you want. If you rush in and assume too quickly, based on your longing and need for love, you may misjudge and misunderstand their intentions. On the other hand, if there are no overt red flags and good feelings emerge based on all your efforts in being observant of others, it's natural to feel your heart pounding with anticipation.

If you think about it, even though you're putting yourself out there in dating arenas, it's still a chance encounter to meet someone terrific. It's a chance that they took by showing up in the same venue. So, you can create your own chance encounters by being present in these venues. Doing so will help you get over any aversions you may have around diversifying your approach to dating. There are actually several ways to meet people when you open yourself up to new ways of meeting people. These methods are all tools for you. So try not to judge them. Instead, look at them as your allies in terms of being able to really meet someone, for that is what counts.

While it may feel great to fantasize about meeting someone in a serendipitous manner, remember that if or when you do meet this other person, it is wise to be utilizing the tools laid out in *The ABCs of Dating*! When you're out in any of these venues mentioned below, be they bars, clubs, the internet and day-to-day life, your personal safety, emotional and physical, comes first. Your task is to create positive dating encounters and get to know someone in a less superficial way.

The odds of meeting another single person are greater than ever. In fact, according to the 2012 Census, if you were standing in a room with 99 other people, forty-one of them would be single. That's a fairly high percentage compared to previous years and decades, leaving you more and more potential partners who are available. However, statistics do not matter as much as your own openness and willingness to make your life work and go for your dating dreams to be realized!

Bars/Nightclubs

Is it possible to meet someone in a bar or nightclub? These are places where people go to unwind and relax and let loose; and yes, it is possible. The big issue here is the presence of alcohol! When alcohol is involved, your judgments and perceptions of others will be impaired. Your longings and needs may run rampant as your inhibitions lessen, but you may not really know whether someone you are talking to is necessarily someone you want to be dating. Agree to begin slowly or at a later date when alcohol isn't involved, unless you are looking for a very casual encounter. People meet in bars, nightclubs and at social events often, so this can be a great way to find someone. There is no need for judgment; if you meet someone and there is a mutual attraction, you can go out at another time, which would count as the actual first date.

Part of the process of dating is about increasing your social circle.

Many nightspots offer fun and themed events. If you enjoy sports, you could attend a sports bar and feel connected to others who share a similar passion. If you love ballroom dancing, many nightclubs host dancing events. You increase the chances of meeting people in these venues. Be flexible and open to enjoy an evening out. You may even develop a new interest while meeting a new community of great people.

The Internet

Social networking websites are a very good way to start researching what you are looking for and seeing if there is anyone out there who appears to be like-minded in many ways. However, I believe social media also needs to be used merely as a beginning tool and a vehicle to see whether or not you want to meet someone in person. You need to be aware that all is not what it seems on paper or in this case...the screen. I would say, "Let the Buyer Beware." One really needs to be curious, cautious and self-protective in a healthy way when you meet complete strangers via the Internet.

With Facebook, Twitter, LinkedIn and other social media sites, it's easier than ever to "research" your date prior to meeting. Doing so has pros and cons and it works both ways because they can research you just as readily. Some profiles, such as on Facebook, have the capability to be blocked to viewers who are "non-friends," while others leave their pages open to the public. If you're dating, whether regularly or not, limit the amount of personal information you make available because people tend to draw conclusions based on what they see and read online. While some of the information can be helpful, ultimately you want to meet someone in person and let them get to know the real you rather than draw conclusions from images and posts. This is why I refer to it as a good place to begin, but that's all it is...a beginning.

Online Dating Sites

Depending on what you are looking for, online dating sites do often yield great results, even though they have a reputation as also being good for casual "hookups." However, safety is always an ever-present part of using this method wisely.

Ask any person if they've tried online dating and you will hear a variety of responses. Some will say, "Yes! That's how I met my spouse!" Some will wince and change the subject because they were negatively impacted by the experience or it yielded no results. Some will say, "I'd never do that in a million years," and tell you their perceptions of why it could never work for them. And, some will say they're currently on one or many dating sites.

These varied responses actually speak to dating methods as a whole. Blind dates would possibly evoke similar responses as meeting someone online. So might speed dating or a blind date. These are just a few examples of the many tools and venues available where you can actively seek a partner, or at the very least a date and each one used will come with pros and cons. If you are open and willing to be out there using one or more of these options, while also using *The ABCs of Dating* as a guide, your odds of success are much greater. Have confidence in yourself and remember, this is not Chemistry homework but creating Chemistry with a new person out there who may be just perfect for you!

Every method of meeting people needs to be considered in a way that would allow dating to occur. When one is open to one method of meeting people and increasing your social circle, other "surprises" may happen like meeting someone unexpectedly, but you have to be out there to meet people to date.

Additionally, the site you join can make a difference in the quality of people you meet. Match.com, eHarmony and other well-known sites, tend to be the most popular for those seeking more serious and committed relationships. A fairly new site, OurTime.com, is geared toward the 50 and over crowd and has become quite popular in that niche. Other sites tend to be geared toward those who are just looking to "hookup" or date casually. Do some online research to get an idea of the ones that might appeal to you. You can also ask friends who have used them which ones worked for them and why.

Find an online dating site or sites that you feel will yield people you want to meet and then go from there.

Most of them will let you browse profiles before signing up. Remember, it is just a tool to ultimately meet in person. The meeting part is essential or all of the work you are doing on yourself would be purely theoretical.

Online Potential

This relatively new and proven method of meeting partners has demonstrated success stories time and again. Match.com states that 1 in 5 relationships start online. Today, that might be conservative. Matchmaking agencies have been putting couples together for years. The internet's version of this method has served as a new, self and tech-driven medium for bringing likeminded couples together.

Having an affordable venue where you can find appropriate people to date means that the door is open to a wider pool of potential dates. Internet dating has also broken down geographical barriers. This is a great feature to many who aren't necessarily looking for someone in their neighborhood. One example of this is someone who is moving to a new town. They can "window" shop the new town online and see what the dating pool looks like. Another example would be someone who lives in a small town and doesn't have many options in their community. By being able to branch out and connect with more people in surrounding or other areas, their chances of meeting new people to date are greatly increased.

Statistically Speaking

Whether you're trying online dating or not, you may read or hear statistics about being single. The ideas in this book will, I hope, motivate you no matter what the "statistics" are! People meet at all ages and stages of life. They fall in love in preschool. They have crushes in elementary school, relationships of one kind or another in high school and in college. Why not continue with what is a developmental urge to meet, connect and possibly fall in love if that is what your heart desires? Certainly, there is a choice here and many are satisfied with their lives as is. But if there is a yearning for love in you, don't be warned off by statistics. Instead, feel proud of yourself for trying to meet and fall in love.

Online Dating Red Flags: Deciphering Potentials from Problems

The reality versus the truth of the people you meet online is an area that needs deciphering. In other words, their profiles may say one thing, but the truth, as you could find out in time, is another.

For instance, if you are looking for a committed relationship that includes marriage, you will need to spend time weeding out those who want to find casual sex versus those who are investing their time and energy online to finding a true partner. Learning to interpret profiles in order to separate the more committed people from the casual ones takes some experience, but with a keen eye, you can get good at it.

We've touched on red flags in earlier chapters and realize they can arise in different stages of a relationship. Red flags can be the little voice in your head that tells you something isn't right. They can also be blatant, physical things, such as a tan line where a wedding ring goes. A red flag can be something you pick up on while someone is talking, like the ex that they're clearly not over. While these are just a few examples of the kinds of red flags that can come up throughout the entire dating process, developing a keen sense of when something is amiss will help you make better choices as you go.

When it comes to online dating, you have to heighten your awareness in other ways. So, what is an example of a red flag in an online dating profile? Let's examine different ways that they can reveal themselves.

A Sparse Profile

A skimpy profile is one form of a potential internet dating red flag. If someone doesn't take the time to tell you about themselves, you need to see it as a potential red flag. You should consider why and ask if you do decide to communicate with them. I agree that some people just don't know what to write on that blank screen or they consider it daunting. That's normal to a degree. Perhaps they assume the rest of their profile, such as their photos, will speak for them instead. However, it's still a potential red flag that they may lack communication skills and the ability or interest to express themselves for who they are.

This could convey a red flag that this issue of insecurity could carry over to their relationship with you.

No In-Person Meeting

An example of a big red flag is when the person avoids meeting you after a handful of back and forth messages and positive communication has been exchanged. If they're encouraging you to continue only by electronic communication, it could be a red flag that they don't want a flesh and blood actual person, but prefer an online buddy. Or maybe they like calling you, but they don't want to arrange a meeting even if it appears to you that it would be safe to meet them for a first date. Remember, online dating is a place to meet people, not to carry out an entire relationship.

Posted Photos

Photographs people post online can reveal a great deal and are an opportunity to get a better sense of who they are. Some things to consider which could raise a red flag might be if the photos are completely dated, or if they are mostly "selfies" or they don't seem to add up to the person they are representing themselves to be. If you have any doubts, trust your instincts and ask questions. For instance, it's sometimes difficult to decipher someone's age especially through a photograph. Ask questions...as long as you do so with good intentions and an open heart.

Other Tips as You Venture the Waters of Online Dating

I highly recommend that you do not text excessively and create a "texting relationship" before meeting in person. Texting may be handy when it comes to the practicalities, such as what time and location to meet, but do not count on this initially as it is likely to create a "faux" connection. People tend to reveal a lot through text messaging and then are surprised when they finally meet the person on the other end of the phone. They can immediately be nonplussed by how much of a stranger the other person feels like in person. Words on a screen are essentially just those...words on a screen. They can raise the excitement, but they don't reflect what the person is really like in person. Of course, once you have been dating regularly, the email, phone call and texting communication tools take on a different meaning and are more relevant. Still, if these methods of communication are your primary methods, rather than sitting down and talking and enjoying one another's company, consider them red flags to what might be a lack of real intimacy in these early stages.

Creating Your Online Profile: Keeping it Positive and Personal

Building a profile online is often the first step to internet dating. It's different from other social networks you may be familiar with because it's primarily for people who *don't* know you yet, whereas other sites, such as Facebook, are for friends and family.

What you write in your profile should reveal who you are, what you enjoy doing and what type of person you would be compatible with. When reading other people's profiles, you'll see that this tends to be the formula that most use. Once you've read a handful of them, you'll have an idea of which kinds of profiles appeal to you and which ones don't.

Keep your own profile positive and honest. Be the one who shows a clear and authentic attitude. Remember, the things you write about in your profile are essentially written out versions of your lists. Think of the things you enjoy doing and others that you hope to do someday such as your bucket list. If you enjoy your friendships and being with family, let them know these are important to you. Do you prefer to go to a concert or a museum or a gallery opening on a Friday night? All of these lifestyle scenarios are worth bringing up so they can learn as much about you as possible to determine if you'd be someone they'd want to date. Naturally, this works both ways as you read other people's profiles.

Upload photos of yourself that show your face, preferably a smiling one and ensure they are current. Try to choose photos that you like as they reflect some authentic aspect of yourself day to day.

When it comes time to initiate contact with someone let them know you took the time to read their profile by including a reference to something they mentioned. Take the time to make each note a personal one. It's important to show that you want to know *them*, so why send a generic note? Also, if the person is interested, this will greatly increase your odds of receiving a positive response. It may also encourage the other person to read your profile more closely and to return the favor of taking the time to mention something specific about you. It's the beginning phase of communication.

Your task then becomes finding out more about them by asking appropriate questions, using your instincts and by being conscious, mindful and aware. Be in the moment and don't get ahead of yourself even if you do feel excited or happy about the person on the screen. You need to go through the A stage of dating starting from the first, to the second and into the third date and beyond, before you jump ahead. A great way to evoke more positive responses from your messages is to pose a question. This is one way to let someone know you took the time to read their profile and expect the same in return. For example, "I too like to take walks on the beach. When was the last time you did this and where was the beach?" Notice if they are responding to your profile by posing questions. You need to trust that questions are ways to become personal despite the fact that this is online communication.

When you feel comfortable and have made contact on the phone, developed a frame of reference for the person that feels legitimate, then you can agree to meet for the first time (we'll talk more about where to meet in Chapter 6). Keep in mind that these are models of friendships you are building. You can be excited but give it the time to develop regardless of attraction, longing and hopefulness.

I'll also note that your goal here is to make a connection that leads to an in-person date and that means making a good impression. Show you care enough about this as an opportunity to meet a real person by sending a real message. It lets others know that you don't skimp when it comes to initiating a date and connection. Ask questions and learn more about him or her. This is someone you might well be compatible with so be open to enjoying the process of learning about another.

Be authentic when you answer their questions. No matter what will be or who they are, at the end of the day, you will respect yourself for doing things right from your end. Eventually, and as you become more experienced at this, you will find that the process can become more pleasant and less disappointing if you are open to just letting some potential people go. In fact, it's best to expect to do so.

It can take time to feel excitement towards someone before the date even occurs. The process is the one you committed to, and just like anything that's worthy, it could take many attempts of doing this and learning to make good choices and use your instincts. This is just one way to help you meet the right people, so don't get discouraged if you don't have immediate results.

Lastly, as you look through profiles and connect with people, keep to your list and being true to what you're looking for. Note the red flags and be ready to move on if someone doesn't seem right. There are many people looking for a great connection and the right one will come along when you let the wrong ones go. Be authentic from the start! That way you will benefit so much more.

Online Dating Safety

With online dating, you are dealing with strangers. Because of this, you need to always put your physical and emotional safety uppermost on your agenda. How do you do this? Observe major red flags and avoid dealing with people who even online are either problematic or overly accommodating. Here are some common sense tips that are worth mentioning:

- Do not give out personal phone numbers until you have followed procedural protocol of the "system" of the dating website you are on. It's designed for compatibility and for your safety.
- Once phone contact has been established, have your list handy and ascertain whether this person has the qualities you might do well with.
- Listen to not only what is being said, but for any potentially alarming communication. You don't have to be hypersensitive, just be aware.
- Be open to having good humor. A spontaneous laugh between two people breaks down barriers and can tell you a lot about someone.
- Don't be afraid to walk away if they're not a match.
- You're in this process to change those old behaviors, so stick to it. Someone better suited to you will come along.
- Always trust your instincts.
- See that your date is willing to meet you in a venue that works for you both and that is public. It's your first meeting and establishing an environment to feel comfortable is necessary.

Speed Dating

Many people enjoy speed dating because it can provide a quick and efficient way for an initial meeting and brief discussion. In as few as five minutes a first impression is made and a potential connection could be had. Everyone is in the same boat as it's been set up in a venue where everyone understands the rules and it often can feel like a great deal of fun. People learn to ask good questions since their time is limited and respond to thoughtful ones just as readily. It's an encapsulated version of getting a sense of mutual attraction and commonalities. Create a list of five questions from your lists, that way you can mix it up and relax and not worry about what you're going to say or ask! Be yourself and recognize that you're all in this together.

It can be a fun dating technique of meeting in a proscribed way. Often people will socialize afterwards and that can create more opportunities for spontaneous meetings.

Now that you're on a new dating journey you're being more open, so even if you do not really connect with anyone, at least you went out. You tried it and possibly made a new friend! If it appears and feels right and safe, it is fine to create a date, at least to meet and begin an assessment of whether you are right for each other. Perhaps you had the chance to chat with one of the other attendees at the event. You could agree to going out to another venue later.

Being social, friendly and open to new experiences can lead to feeling better about yourself. So again, affirm yourself for trying a different method, no matter the outcome.

Real Life - Spontaneous vs. Intended Meetings

Sometimes when you're out and about living your life, going to the gym or the grocery store, you might just meet someone. Of course most people have romantic fantasies of meeting the love of their life through organic ways. Usually this type of fateful encounter feels exciting as there often is a physical and tangible attraction right away. Whilst it's great to start there, remember one method of meeting is no better or worse than the other as long as a quality relationship is the end goal and result.

Though there may be a connection right from the start, you still need to stay keenly aware since you really don't know the person yet. You have the tools and ability to set boundaries and a good use of instincts to notice any red flags. So enjoy yourself and trust yourself to be able to be open to a chance at love or whatever type of relationship you were hoping for.

The Proverbial "Blind Date"

Blind date referrals can come about from friends, family and business associates. Even though blind dates are not favored by all, there are plenty of uplifting stories about successful couples who met this way.

However, keep in mind that whilst their intentions may be genuine and good, you should ask them why they expect you two to get along. Do they know what you are looking for? Do they know enough about the other person too? Express your needs and desires that are on your list clearly. You do not have to show them your actual list, but refer to it when you are telling them about the type of person you are looking for. Otherwise you might be left wondering if they really considered the qualities of both of you or if they simply wanted to set someone up on a whim.

If it's your desire to go on a blind date, remember that it is ultimately up to you to do the assessment of the person without being overly reliant on your friends' choices. You are going to be the one in any relationship, so only choose to go out with someone whom you are interested in getting to know and whom may have the qualities you are looking for in a partner. In order to decide this, before the date, find out as much as you can about the other person from your matchmaking friend. For example, if you learned they are still hurting from a recent divorce or have been married and divorced five times or anything else that appears to be a red flag, you'll know to pass. It is perfectly okay to politely decline if it's obviously not going to be a good match for you. This then frees you up to spend your time focusing on who else could be available.

No matter how you meet your blind date, be it through mutual friends or online social networking sites, ultimately *The ABCs of Dating* process is the same. You have to find the right person for *you* and feel a connection between the two of you. In other words, Cupid's arrow has to strike for you! No matter how you meet, you also have to get to know a person so you can make a rational assessment by using your heart and your head.

If you are set up by a friend or colleague, it's important again to ask them why they feel the two of you would get along well. Sometimes they may just be doing a favor to a friend and haven't really thought much about the two people they're introducing or whether or not they are really suited for each other. Although it's good to be open, it's important to ask your friend questions about this person they want you to meet. What similarities are there in lifestyle and personality? What qualities do they possess that makes your friend recommend them so highly? Dig deeper to get answers ahead of time so you know you are about to meet a quality person, whether there are sparks or not.

If it sounds like a suitable matching, be sure you and the other person talk on the phone before you meet. This way it may be a blind date but you are making it your own experience.

Friends often know each other extremely well. They can have a great sense that you and the date might well make for a good couple. They might just be right, so be open to the possibility, give it a try and thank them for their thoughtfulness.

Chapter Summary:

No one method of meeting someone is really better than another. You may have a preference to engage in speed dating rather than online dating. You may prefer meeting people naturally through life and being out and about. Online dating, speed dating events, blind dates, networking, meet-ups and day to day life, are all opportunities for you to meet people and to achieve your goals in your love life. If you are indeed serious about meeting someone, remember that each method carries an opportunity for you to be "in the field," in the dating arena with actual dates, not longings or virtual experiences.

This is about the reality of growing, learning and practicing all that you've learned and continue to learn about yourself. There can be no real failures if seen in this light. You will enhance your experiences in meeting people, practice your social skills and learn much about others. It's a chance for you to nurture the hope and dream that there is something special in someone you may have met through any of the methods above. More importantly, you are honoring your longing for love by doing so.

Happiness, not in another place but this place
not for another hour
but this hour.
–Walt Whitman

Chapter 6: On the Date

If I am not worth the wooing, I am surely not worth the winning
—Henry Wadsworth Longfellow

Deciding to Go on a Date

By now, you have spent time determining if you want to meet each other and have decided you do. Naturally, you want to make the most of each date. After all, you are investing the time and energy to meet after you've done the necessary leg work to decide that it feels like the right step. Doubt and ambivalence should not be present; at the same time, nervous anticipation is normal.

Excitement is a positive emotion and it's wonderful to anticipate getting to know a person. For now you have one meeting arranged, but of course, should it go well, you obviously hope for another and possibly more. No one can ever know for sure what will be. This well could be your future life partner or it could be a first and last date, but at least you're going out and making progress. So, go with a clear mind, enjoy yourself, and remember that there is no point in getting ahead of yourself with your dreams and your longings. They are important to have and cherish and hold dear to your heart; however, you need to live in the moment.

There is meaningful work to be done in determining who this person is. Whether it is a meeting that doesn't occur and leaves disappointment, whether it is a one-time meeting or whether this person turns out to be the person of your dreams and you of his or hers is all part of the journey you cannot anticipate from your current, in the moment, vantage point.

Picking a Place for a Great First Date

Ideally, the two of you have agreed on a place that feels right for you both. Even in the process of choosing this place, there was an opportunity to be mindful as to whether or not your date was interested in having both of you contribute to the decision. You can ask yourself: *Was the decision purely about convenience for him or her? Did they choose it without involving you in the decision? Did they call, text, or email you about where and when to meet? Did you let it be known that you would prefer to talk on the phone beforehand?* (Note: I always recommend a phone call above other methods, as it is the best initial screening and hearing a voice is so much more personal. Talking to someone on the phone, where character can start to shine through, can tell you a lot about the person before you meet.) Answering these questions will give you some insight into the characteristics of your date.

Let's assume all of this went easily and you are looking forward to your date. You are excited and revved up as the person you met online or briefly out and about in the world, is someone you feel you may get along well with. They are someone you get a sense of authenticity about and feel that you will be safe in meeting, somewhere outside your home or neighborhood. Because so many people naturally do this, I must add that researching someone online or checking them out on Facebook does not constitute knowing them. That only happens in person through conversation, interactions and observations on your initial meeting and the others that may come.

Maintaining a Balanced Conversation

There are essential social skills needed to be a natural conversationalist. By getting out there and dating, you are learning about how comfortable you are becoming with interactions during a date. Of course you might have some anxiety, but it is healthy and refreshing to admit to your date that you are feeling nervous or excited about meeting especially if you feel overwhelmed to the point where it's getting in your way of engaging. There is plenty to enjoy and observe when you meet someone new. This time together is about being your authentic self with boundaries, as it's a first meeting, so they can get to know you and you them.

You have your list in your head, but try not to spend too much time thinking about it. Save that for later assessment. Learn about this person, observe who they seem to be and see if you are enjoying yourself. Be who you are and avoid hyperbole or trying to analyze what you think he or she may be thinking. If in doubt, ask! That's what questions are there for and you are there to get to know each other and be comfortable doing so. One of the hallmarks of being genuine and sincere is in the feeling that you are truly safe to be yourself...so why not start that trend at the beginning? Certainly first date jitters can lead to some awkward conversations. Basic social skills are a necessity and so is the ability to have a normal conversation. Making a real attempt to get to know a person is imperative. Shyness and awkward moments are normal, too. Keep in check with yourself and see if there are points of interest in general and specifically between you and your date. Ask and answer questions with ease and have fun with this initial meeting. In a friendly tone, you can ask questions about their lives, background, family, work, hobbies and interests. You are not on a job interview, nor is this an interrogation. It should be fun and interesting to learn about each other.

Take note of what you are asked and to the answers given when you ask questions. This is a chance for deeper listening, for potential red flags to be noticed and to observe your own reactions. You may not be initially attracted to your date, but you might as well use all dates as an opportunity to engage, whether you think there may be a second date or not.

In addition, keep these thoughts in mind:
- Are times of silence comfortable for you and the person you are meeting?
- Are you both desperately trying to cover them with too much chatter?
- Are you anxious and if so, what are you anxious about?

If any of these come up as a *yes* for you, consider this: you might be surprised about how being sincere helps from the start. Try to focus less on the need to reveal yourself quickly or feel that there is some pre-ordained script and focus more on having an enjoyable time.

Stay in the moment and don't worry so much about how they feel about you or whether or not you're making the right impression, as you will be practicing the ideas put out in this book. If you can do this, you'll be able to relax and be yourself.

Alternatively, insecurities can be overwhelming and could thwart your ability to think about your own responses and your sense of this person. This is where the A phase really pays off. Start from a point of understanding about what works for you and learn and get to know this person you are spending time with. Relax and be yourself!

Often people who are very ready for the right person and are serious about seeing if this person fits their mold, may ask more questions earlier on. Don't be unnerved. It may be their way of showing you they care about themselves. There is room for reality. No one is constantly upbeat, perfect, or without issues, life history, or painful experiences. It's how comfortable you are with the narrative of your own life that counts. Don't see yourself through another's eyes, especially in a negative light, and thus predetermining that you will be found lacking. Your insecurities may bother you personally, but they may not affect how someone else sees you. In other words, do not do the work of "rejection" for another. Have your self-esteem and enjoy being yourself and again, relax and just listen, learn and be pleased that you are there.

Listen with a Keen Ear

Listen to what the person you're out with is saying. As you do so, try to get a sense of who they are by noticing the following:
- *Do they appear to be authentic or are they over compensating or trying to impress?*
- *Do they listen and ask questions of you in a balanced fashion?*
- *Do they appear to know why they are dating and what they may need in a partner?*
- *Do they seem ready to be dating or are they overly guarded or overly forward?*
- *Do they speak kindly of others?*

Now is the time to listen for and be aware of blatant and or subtle red flags. It's always a good idea to pay attention to how your date treats and interacts with others you encounter. Take note if they tend to be rude to the valet or coat check person, for example, or overly attentive to a server at the restaurant. These actions are a good indication of how they treat people and can also be received as dismissive toward you, such as in the case of extra attention given to the server.

All these are red flags for you to evaluate. Hopefully, having an impolite or domineering person is not on your lists of essential or ideal qualities!

Another example is if someone orders several drinks before the appetizer. Do not make excuses for them, such as thinking they are nervous. Their behavior has meaning and do not be afraid to ask or inquire, when appropriate, as to what this means. At the very least, make a mental note of the behavior. It could well be a red flag and you may not want to be dealing with an overly anxious person or a person who drinks too much.

However, also listen to the qualities you have listed as desirable for you. Do they seem kind, a good person and someone you find yourself drawn to? You are listening and learning about them and remember to appreciate the positive qualities you can sense in them.

Paying Attention to Incompatibilities

Incompatibilities are sometimes overlooked or simply not obvious early on. If you find your date very attractive or charismatic, it's easy to get caught up in their presence and to let incompatibilities go without notice. This is when being alert and present makes a difference.

Incompatibilities come in varying degrees, which is where your list and allowances start to come into play. For example, a possible source of incompatibility may be if they have a family from a prior marriage. If you are fine with this, that is great. However, within that constellation, think about where, how and if you would fit in. Is their relationship with their children and ex a healthy one or do they have a lot of concerns and duress from an ex or from children that would carry over into your relationship? Why not discover now rather than going along with someone else's situation only to find out in a few months that it's just not working for you?

There are so many things that emerge in people and in their histories as time unfolds. You want a real person with thoughts, longings, dreams and disappointments and those who have dealt with real life losses and setbacks. But it is how people address these events that are a part of their narrative that make you feel comfortable or make you wonder if this is a "red flag."

For instance, in a disastrous and shifting economy, there have been major setbacks, loss of jobs, income and insecurities or need for new ventures. This is never an easy subject to address. The more honest and heartfelt you both are, the more normalizing real life experiences become and you should find yourself connecting in a more truthful way even though you are on a first or second date. Maybe if someone had an influential position, but subsequently had to take on a lower paying and less important position, you might find yourself admiring their ability to adapt and not care about the millions they lost or could have made! Their flexibility and true values will impress you more as will their resiliency.

Don't project and think for another. Instead, reveal who you are and your life circumstances and ask them directly what they are looking for. You may be surprised to find that many people are looking for honesty and truthfulness.

During the early-on dates, you have a chance to assess basic values while having fun doing so. Doing this with an open mind makes it so much more meaningful for you. When and if feelings evolve, these experiences and thoughts you had upon first meeting will be something you will both later reflect on and reminisce about.

Express What You Are Feeling

On the date, you are learning about your own feelings and reactions. Sometimes people expect the worst and they are so nervous. Then the opposite happens and they find themselves confused and getting in their own way. What if, for instance, they find themselves very attracted to someone that they can barely focus on listening to them? The list they worked hard on writing goes out the window and composure has been lost. There is the surprise aspect of such attraction, and if you find that you cannot concentrate on even thinking or assessing, what do you do? It may be helpful to say something about this so you can become a bit more level headed and be less distracted by pure physical attraction. You could say that you didn't expect them to be so much better looking in person than in their photo. You could take a breath and realize that this might be a quality on your list that you didn't expect. Note that it is just one part of a person and who they are. Why not pay a compliment and say you like their looks, their appearance, if this is clearly on your mind? You need to be calm enough on all levels and not thrown by your own reactions. It's important to stay in that observant, present and mindful place. If you are feeling connected and attracted and drawn to someone in many areas that you feel a kinship with, it's fine to let them know that you are enjoying getting to know them. It's okay to say that you felt nervous, anxious and excited about meeting them, especially if it helps you to feel more comfortable. A little bit of humility is a good thing. Rather this than relying solely on cocktails to free and loosen your inhibitions to express yourself!

Be Discreet and Have Boundaries

Everyone has the proverbial "baggage," but do you have to reveal it or hear about it on your first date? If the person sitting opposite you has a need to reveal how successful they are in bed or how many conquests they have had, consider this a red flag. Do not assume they will be any different with you before moving on to the next person and you become another piece of their history and part of the storyline on their next coffee date.

The need to reveal all instantly is childlike and more of a confessional. The tendency to do this is an underlying need to seek approval from another. However, if you do ask a question, it's important to listen to and interpret the response and learn about their personal narrative. This is an opportunity to see how well you can get to know and understand them. Determining appropriate boundaries is a hallmark of a mature person, whereas revealing all often means a lack of distinction and emotional maturity. It is true that some things need to be shared in the spirit of getting to know someone and to gauge truthfulness later. For instance, if the person you just met is currently separated from a spouse, then that qualifies as an important bit of information to reveal. This would allow you to take into consideration whether that's a situation you're prepared to cope with and if it would impact your relationship. In this case, you would need to assess where they are in this situation and if they are in a positive place to let you in and move forward.

Every issue and life situation is idiosyncratic, so one

cannot always generalize that something is a red flag without exploring it further. They too will be assessing your vulnerabilities and losses and whether or not the two of you are compatible. But do not worry as whoever you are with will be seeing that you are in the moment, open and happy and that will be more important than your past. Being an integrated person makes you human and interesting! Embrace and accept your past and be ready and happy in the present to experience all that life has to offer regarding potential love.

The Reaction to a Direct Question is as Important as the Answer

If you have curiosity about someone, which is important, and you ask them a question, be sure to take note of how they react. Is it with great discomfort? Are they overly glib or is it an authentic response? Are they open by saying they feel awkward answering, but understand the need for you to ask a specific question? If they squirm around, avoid eye contact, or avoid the subject without clearly setting a healthy boundary for its discussion, see this as fishy and a red flag. In some cases, it may be that they're shy, which means you have to ascertain which one it is: are they naturally introverted or avoiding intentionally? Perhaps it's too early or too personal of a question to answer, but, if so, this should be communicated simply and respectfully.

Alternatively, if your date answers your somewhat personal question by divulging too much information, this can also be a red flag as well. Yes, they may feel comfortable with you, but there should be a pacing of unfolding of information that feels natural and comfortable to both of you. Giving too much personal information on the first date could overwhelm the other person and vice versa. If this happens to you, you may not feel comfortable asking further questions for fear of too much more information being divulged, and hence the conversation becomes awkward. You do not want your date to become your time of unloading burdens, even if they are a good listener. This is an unfolding, a sharing and an opportunity to be in the company of someone you just met. The very nature of that is simple and alive enough. It's okay to just enjoy this part of dating and not see this as a performance or as work.

Another possibility is that your date answers the question with just enough information without letting you know more about them. This could build an interest and pique curiosity about them, while at the same time creating a boundary. Ideally, they will pose a similar question in return and a natural conversation will flow. If they're comfortable and respectful in answering pointed questions, this is a good sign that they have emotional maturity. You may want to evaluate the level of openness. Remember that good communication is very likely a quality on your list. When you encounter positive communication, be sure you acknowledge it. It's great for you to feel you are getting what you need and desire. How someone responds to a question is important if you like them and are interested in getting to know them better. This becomes an opportune time to ask questions about things you are interested in learning about them. For instance, how they like their career or their interests. If they are still connected to an ex-spouse or significant other is important to assess, especially if the conversation about someone else keeps coming up. How open they are to letting you know is helpful to learn. Maybe they weren't aware they were talking so frequently about their previous relationship. They may not be conscious of the fact that it communicates a sense of involvement in their past. You are not there to wait for a perfect person but someone who is flesh and blood and comes with real life experience, who has a good enough handle on their narrative and on themselves to self-reflect and respond to you. These are the ingredients to create trust and emotional safety necessary for love to develop and unfold.

Chapter Summary:

On your dates remember to be your natural self and maintain a balanced conversation. Listen with a "third ear" of reason and take note of not only the red flags but the green light to go ahead too. Don't be afraid to ask about previous relationships, sexual history and previous dating experiences. However, pace yourself and be initially circumspect in answering. The details are not first date topics and communication needs to build over time. Express your feelings and thoughts openly and spontaneously and be authentic, even when nervous.

As you're talking, notice how your date responds to a direct question because how they do so is as important as the answer itself.

If things are progressing well and you are having a good time, savor this. You have embarked on dating and getting to know someone. Enjoy it.

Chapter 7: A's: Sex

Your body needs to be held and to hold, to be touched and to touch. None of these needs is to be despised, denied, or repressed. But you have to keep searching for your body's deeper need, the need for genuine love. Every time you are able to go beyond the body's superficial desires for love, you are bringing your body home and moving toward integration and unity.
—*Henri Nouwen*

Attraction and Compatibility

So what about physical attraction? It is a wonderful, life-affirming spark, emboldening people and inspiring poets throughout history. Let's look at the role of attraction, passion, lust and sex and see how they belong in the dating and early relationship world. Right off the bat, yes they belong and chemistry and attraction are part of this alchemy.

Some of the more conservative cultures and people, who for example have, as a staple of their culture, arranged marriages, are encouraged to focus on the emotional qualities of a person first. They expect and encourage a level of holding off on acting on physical impulses until a commitment is made, usually by marriage. This is the situation with religious people who feel that it is vital to have sex established after an emotional or legal commitment, such as marriage, has occurred.

Although this approach may not be for everyone, there is wisdom to its tenets. It's a process that allows people to continue to acknowledge that physical attraction is present, but keeps a focus on assessing emotional compatibility, allowing sex to be a natural and healthy part of the emotional intimacy that has developed over time. Later on, after the commitment is made, a couple may find that sexual issues and difficulties, if there are any, will need to be addressed and the sexual part of the relationship made stronger and more vibrant. This is part of any healthy, living breathing relationship and worth dealing with.

However, in mainstream culture, different elements arise such as sex being included early on in the process of getting to know someone. In this chapter, we address many of these.

Here are some questions to consider:
- *What are the emotional consequences of jumping towards sexual activity before you really know the person or their motivation for dating?*
- *When and is there a Right Time to have sex?*
- *When is it Appropriate Timing to Ask Sex Related Questions?*
- *How Much Does Intimacy Contribute to Closeness?*

Emotional Consequences

Emotional consequences are especially important to consider if you are not looking for the proverbial "hookup" but instead desire a more complete relationship that includes sexuality but doesn't depend on it. Before sex enters your relationship consider these quandaries: *What can it teach you if sex occurs early on in a relationship? How does it affect or confuse things? Does it create a sense of premature or false intimacy? What if you are part of an "open relationship" where you are a same sex or heterosexual union that allows for casual "hookups" outside of the primary relationship?*

In open relationships there are unique and discreet issues that arise regarding sexuality. These can be both emotional and physical. Consequences to open relationships can include jealousy and hurt and, in the nature of the physical, exposure to sexuality transmitted diseases.

So it's important to understand that the nature of the sexual relationship is enhanced by parameters set honestly and with clarity by couples even if their model of fidelity does not include monogamy. Some people I've worked with, for example, may see this as part of their relationship and do not feel that outside sex impacts that primary relationship. For others, outside engagements may threaten the very foundation of the couple. For many couples, sex outside the primary relationship can be very damaging to the integrity of the primary connection. It may even lead to the end of a relationship or marriage. Every couple starting out needs to determine their truth to maintain the needs they have for a relationship that works for them.

As this chapter is about posing pertinent questions and exploring them for yourself, think about all of these questions to see how they impact you in early dating. We will cover young, the middle aged and the elderly, same sex people and heterosexual people, people from all different walks of life and cultures and preexisting attitudes about sex and the role of intimacy in dating, early relationships and building the foundation for love.

When and is there a Right Time? The "Right Time" should be the right time for you! There are no rules to when the right time is. But there are consequences to all actions and generally speaking, being comfortable and ready greatly enhances the intimacy of a sexual relationship right from the start. It's better to wait and feel emotionally safe and enjoy sensuality and fun, than rushing premature sex to "get it out the way" or feel pressured.

Having sex very early on in the dating process, for example in the A Phase of *The ABCs of Dating*, may not lead to the growth of a relationship especially if you're wanting a long term commitment. Having sex early on can tell you whether or not there is a mutual attraction and that you may be physically compatible; however, it does not validate that you can be genuinely close nor does it mean you have a real and authentic intimacy. Those deeper layers cannot be gained without spending actual time together. Only quality time spent together can foster genuine intimacy between two people.

Early sexual activity can create the feeling of forced intimacy in the relationship as a whole. Sexual encounters that produce false intimacy can mean that you are having good sex together but can also leave you feeling awkward and uncomfortable with each other in social settings or amongst friends or even on a formal date. In addition, be sure you are not unconsciously using sex as a way to actively create a pseudo-intimacy so as not to engage in a real way emotionally. Check in if you have fears of intimacy—if you do, you may need to focus on finding a way to feel safer and open up. Think about your fears of intimacy and what they entail. Are they related to abandonment issues, or trauma or fear of hurt? This is a great time to grow, learn and be patient with yourself. If you take the time now, there can be many benefits to having this work lead you to great sex in a developing relationship and beyond.

Perhaps you are using sex to create an illusion of affection, as you may have a longing to merge with someone before you really know them. It could stem from loneliness, the need to be held, to get a hug and to kiss. A mutually satisfying sexual relationship could develop if you just relaxed and allowed it to take a more natural course. As you may be looking for affection but are mistrustful about finding it, you jump into a familiar pattern, becoming sexually available very quickly without your heart connected to a person you have taken the time to know.

Some people may be proving how desirable they are without allowing someone to discover this for themselves by jumpstarting a relationship sexually and without letting the other person learn that there is more to them than externals and an ability to seduce easily. In other words, don't sell yourself short out of impatience or longing. Self-esteem and self–worth *do* count. Waiting until you are comfortable and sharing with your partner that you want to have sex as a part of an ongoing, emotionally rewarding relationship before becoming sexual is not a deal breaker! And if it is, this is not the person for you.

As dating is very personal, idiosyncratic and individualized, the timing and the role of sex is something for you to consider. It's good to lead up to sexual intimacy by flirting, kissing, holding and sharing feelings before diving in, so to speak. Everyone feels vulnerable about the need for validation or approval but engaging in sex prematurely can exacerbate deeper issues that are present for you—or block the pathway to real and honest conversation.

Ask Questions Before You Leap

At some point, it's important to ask what having sex means to you both before you leap into action. An important criterion to find out is how many other people, if any, is the person you are dating sexually active with. Are you comfortable with the possibility that they are not just having sex with you? Though this is a sensitive topic, it's important to be open and honest about what you want to find out about your partner's sexual habits. Remember that it is your right to ask. Secrets aren't sexy!

It is always better to ask and discuss than to act first and talk about it later, as by then it is too late to go back. The best approach is to determine the top few things that you need to know from a new partner in order to feel comfortable. The questions below are ones that I have noted in my practice as a psychotherapist over the years. Note that the answers to questions you will have for your partner might not all emerge in one conversation. They could unfold over time and they don't need to be asked all at once if you're not sexually active with them yet.

These sample questions are part of an introductory conversation and meant to be done comfortably; it's not an interrogation, but your way of communicating with and learning about your partner:

- *Are you sexually engaged with others? Do you always practice safe sex?*
- Are you HIV positive? Do you have HPV, herpes, or any other STD?
- Do you use condoms?
- Are you only interested in "hooking up" sexually or are you available for a more complete relationship?
- Is sexual exclusivity important to you?

As safety on all levels has been highlighted in this book, it is important to stay safe and healthy—sexually as well as emotionally. In moving forward, it's important to ask questions that make the connection more honest and you more comfortable.

If you have an STD, are HIV positive, or have herpes it's vitally important to be open and to reveal this information even if your new partner doesn't ask. It should be at the forefront of your sexual conversations. You may want to share when or if you were tested. You need to be responsible and truthful and let the chips fall where they may. If the other person is not comfortable with any aspect of your history (or vice versa), it's better to find out early on. At the very least you can be friends and nothing is lost. At the best, you may like each other more, warts and all (no pun intended!) and find a way to practice the best safe sex.

When it comes to couples where pregnancy can occur, there is a need for discussion regarding contraception which certainly needs to be had very early on before engaging sexually.

The issues for middle aged people are different and unique. Insecurities abound at every life stage, but maybe even more so as age creeps up. Middle aged people tend to fear not looking as good unclothed or feel concerned about being "out of practice" if they've been devoid or starved of intimacy and sexuality.

In this stage and in older people, there are other special issues. For example, women are menopausal or post-menopause and fear dryness or lack of arousal and with men there may be possible fears of arousal and performance issues. If there are sexual dysfunctions that have been present for you before, don't be afraid to talk openly with your future partner. Chances are they share similar insecurities regarding their age and an open conversation can lead to a good laugh—or fireworks in the bedroom.

A deep emotional connection can enhance a sexual connection greatly. Why not try? These situations are part of the aging process. You are not a machine, but a human being experiencing each of life's tumultuous stages. You need to enjoy being present in every stage of your life, full of insecurities at times but also full of promise.

Many older people still compare their middle-aged or even elderly bodies to the bodies they had in their youth. As people age physically, they continue to grow emotionally and change is a normal, natural and beautiful part of life. As such, it's important and healthy to embrace and be fully present and engaged in every stage of life.

It's important to keep in mind that sensuality, playfulness and evolving sexuality include the heart as well as the body.

In some cases, sex can be an activity without feeling or soul, but sex can also be a creative force and sensual part of people connecting in their current truth, whatever that may be.

Intimacy Counts

In all the relationships mentioned, ranging from heterosexual to same sex to the young, middle aged and elderly, the question I pose that is central to all: *To what degree do sex and intimacy converge?* The happiest couples are often the ones who merge all of the necessary components of a relationship: reality, romance, sexuality, feelings of affection and love. Love and sex are two separate drives and needs which can, in the best case, merge into a cohesive relationship. It is up to each individual couple to determine whether they are compatible emotionally and sexually. It is also up to each couple to discover how their unconscious longings and fantasies are connected. It takes risk and adventure to develop and share as intimacy unfolds.

Even though many are hoping it will be, sex is not an Olympic sport! It should be a comfortable part of an evolving sense of connection that works for both you and your partner. Even if it's your wedding night and you're in an arranged marriage, the buildup to intimacy needs to be real. The sexual intimacy between you may have happened after an appropriate preamble leading to it in the A or B Phase of dating. It is part of the emotional climate. It is supposed to be pleasurable. It is not a performance but an extension of the whole person that you are and should be integrated in your sincerity about being yourself and being comfortable and honest with your partner.

If you take Viagra for a kick start if you are a man, or whether you need lubrication or a hormonal prescription or natural remedy if you are a woman, wait until you are emotionally comfortable with your mate so that you feel safe enough to address these concerns. It is about ultimately feeling happy, in time and space, no matter your age, background or culture. Sharing intimacy means being yourself with another person, purely and simply. It means feeling confident, happy and alive. You may feel active and find yourself tidying and fixing your home, dousing yourself in aromatic soaps, or finding candles and music that create a sensual and romantic atmosphere. Whatever it is, you create a fun and safe space that is exciting and enlivening for you to enjoy the unfolding of sex with your partner. Sexuality and sensuality keep people feeling vibrant and connected to their best selves. Be fearless when dating to address concerns and reveal yourself honestly and truthfully.

When the sex works on all levels, and the affection and love and goals are compatible, then the sexual relationship can be ever-present in the equation of a beautiful relationship. Love and sex, hand in hand, under one bright umbrella, is what you are going for!

Chapter Summary:

Consenting to a sexual encounter or adding sex to an existing relationship ought not to be done until a discussion on history, expectations and any issues is had. Though some people will feel comfortable having sex early on in a relationship, doing so is unlikely to tell you very much about the person other than whether or not you are sexually compatible. If, instead, you integrate the sex whilst the relationship has time to blossom on an emotional level, the results will be more rewarding and most likely longer lasting. Couples who let the anticipation build while getting to know one another can lead to a more rewarding sexual life and lustful experiences together in safety and fun.

In any relationship, you should always feel

comfortable talking to the other person about birth control, sexually transmitted diseases, or any related issues around sexuality. A mature relationship means that if you are having sex with someone, you should feel comfortable having these conversations. If you don't, it is likely too soon in the relationship to be sexually active. Remember, real sensuality develops in the B and C stage of dating, not in the A stage. If you do not trust the answers you are receiving, take your time and get to know the person longer. Also, take time to address your own mistrust so that eventually it feels right for you to let go and enjoy.

      Different age groups will encounter their own unique aspects to a sexual relationship. Younger generations need to be safe with contraception to avoid unwanted pregnancies and STDs. Middle aged and elderly couples are often concerned about body image and performance and even physical comfort. Ideally, you will find a partner with whom you can discuss these things openly and honestly. And remember to be compassionate to both yourself and to your partner, and, of course, to be unabashedly yourself in lust.

Chapter 8: A's: After the Date

That Love is all there is, is all we know of Love.
—Emily Dickenson

In *The ABCs of Dating*, it is important to reflect upon the time spent on your date after it has ended. Whether what has occurred was a great success, a great disappointment or somewhere in between, analysis is vital. Analysis does not mean to pick it apart hurtfully, but to do so with clarity, honesty and objectivity as an attempt to see and discover what you have learned about another and about yourself. By putting yourself out there in the dating world, you have decided that it is the right time in your life to be out looking. Now it is a matter of finding the right person who also feels it is the right time in *their* life to be exploring and looking for a fulfilling relationship. Being emotionally ready and being ready at a time in your life when you desire a relationship are important factors in finding the right person. Timing and readiness count as when a person isn't desirous of an intimate relationship, or mature enough to handle one, this will be a factor in possibly not allowing for a successful relationship.

Remember to be objective and calm, for this one date is not the only possibility you will ever have. Try to assuage that fear as it could cloud your objectivity. Dating takes time and practice. Making friends doesn't happen overnight. The model is not that different. It's an unfolding relationship beginning with a first date.

After your date think it over and ask yourself:
- *Does this person meet any of your Essentials from your list?*
- *Do they share your ideals?*
- *Have you gone back to your list and evaluated this person against your experience?*
- *Were there any red flags and did you make note of them at the time or later?*
- *Did you enjoy the process of getting to know each other?*
- *Did they seem to enjoy the process of finding out about you?*
- *Did the conversation seem balanced?*
- *Do you remember the date clearly or did you drink so much that it's hard to remember with clarity?*

These may all seem like a lot to ask, but most of the answers will likely come quickly.

It's important to be as mindful as possible in this process. When you go back and look at your list, think about how you've arrived at this point in your journey and all the clarity you've achieved. If your list and your new perspective don't line up with the person who sat at the table across from you, be willing to move on. Many people report months or even years later that they saw all the signs that first night. They saw the red flags but still dove in, head-first. Think about those times when you saw the cues and red flags but ignored them, only to realize they impacted the relationship.

After the date, especially if it went well, there are more questions to be asked:
- *Did you decide mutually to see each other again?*

- *Did you communicate your decision clearly and assertively?*
- *Was it with a sense of delight and positive enthusiasm or were you ambivalent?*

You may need another date and more time together to decide whether or not you like each other enough to continue dating. Be direct and communicate this to them if you would like more time. It's a great quality to care enough for yourself, but it's also important that your partner does too. Recognizing that there is a connection or lack of one is an early step in dating. Anyone who is serious about the idea of developing a real, true connection will also try to figure out whether you are right for each other or not, whether you have found the magic that is so enticing and overwhelmingly great, and whether you share a resonance of life goals. A second date could help you decipher whether or not both of you are really ready for what you feel you want. This takes time together to truly ascertain. If all feels good and aligns in a positive way, you will likely choose to continue to see each other and the beginning of a relationship could blossom.

How Long Does the A Phase Last?

People often ask me how long the A stage lasts. How many dates? Is one date enough? Two? Five? My answer is to think about your personal life situations. Such thinking happens in other areas in our life, so why not in dating? An example would be whether or not to rent or to buy a home or apartment. You would not view the home only once before deciding to buy it—sight unseen could lead to a catastrophe of judgment. It's best to go see the house and neighborhood at different times of day so you can get a clear picture of it. There are elements to decide on before making an offer, such as location, heating and cooling, the noise level in the neighborhood throughout the day and night, the smells, the general safety, the neighbors themselves and many other aspects on your list.

The same kind of thoughtfulness would be appropriate for a job interview. It's common to be interviewed more than once by several people for a job. *What does the company culture feel like? What will your opportunities for growth be like?* You will evaluate these questions through time and communication. You will want to ask questions and your potential employer will likewise engage with you in a similar fashion. Going into the interview, you are both hoping this will be a good fit, but it takes time and evaluation from both sides before you can really know. Utilize these examples of determining what you long for with practical considerations in dating. You are talking about the kinds of choices that are important for your well-being and that lead to romance and happiness. Trust your instincts, your attraction and your thoughts about where this could lead you to in your love life!

When Do You Tell People You Have Met Someone?

Consider that it may actually take several dates before you begin to move into the flow of things within the relationship. During this dating process, be aware and conscious of whom you share your feelings and experiences with, especially early on. Your mother, sister, brother or envious friend may judge or confuse your experience with their own hidden agenda. For some, keeping your dating life on the private side works. For others, it's helpful to share their feelings about the date. There are no set in stone rules. *The ABCs of Dating* can help you figure things out as to what works for you. When dating advice and feedback doesn't come from the best place from family and friends, it is a good idea to find a neutral party to talk to. Otherwise, you may hear things like, "you're being too 'fussy' or 'choosy,'" and other comments that can make you doubt your own instincts and undermine or sabotage the progress you're making through utilizing *The ABCs of Dating*. If you need someone to talk to, consider seeking professional advice.

I love meeting people who reach out at this stage. Everyone can use support when evaluating what is right for them and what is not. A good therapist is a neutral party who knows what you are striving towards and can help get you there. I find that I support people by understanding their goals and working openly to see that nothing is unconsciously blocking their clear evaluation and assessments. Plus, it's great to have encouragement through all stages of this process.

Check-in Questions:
Now is a great time to take some time to stop, check-in and reflect on your dates.
Here are some things to consider:
- *Have you varied the venues of your dates?*
- *Have you met during the day and done something different from your usual dating practices? Have you visited a museum, taken a walk or explored a different area?*
- *Are you compatible in terms of day to day lifestyle?*
- *Do you share interests that allow for interesting dates that are mutually enjoyable?*

By asking these questions and many others you are evaluating fluidity and ease from a place of normalcy which will help you to see things more clearly. As a relationship progresses, people tend to loosen up; it causes them to be less on their "best behavior," so to speak. That doesn't mean anything bad, per se, because it means that they are becoming more natural, relaxed and at ease. This is all part of the progression from the A Phase to the B Phase and needs to be experienced. Dating does not take place in a vacuum but as a part of your entire life. Think about how the date made you feel and if you are looking forward to seeing this person again. Do you feel you have benefited by meeting this person? Think about dating as a part of the reality of your life and not as such a separate activity from general socializing. As more dates happen and more closeness develops, you are evaluating if this is part of the transition from the A Phase to the B Phase of dating which probably leaves you feeling excited, a little afraid and happy.

This is where real intimacy begins to develop, bringing with it more opportunity for you to be aware and mindful and to ask more informed questions. For instance:
- *Is there contact with each other between arranged dates?*
- *Has it become sexual? Do you feel romantic when you are together with your partner?*
- *Are you ignoring the red flags?*
- *Are you own issues of anxiety, neediness or fear of being hurt or abandoned stirring up?*

The issues were addressed already in the earlier chapters about preparing yourself for dating but are worth reevaluating at any phase so that your personal growth can continue.

Once a good beginning to a relationship is established, couples will want to move forward with exclusivity. This should be a mutually decided step. If this describes you and your partner, then you are on your way to the B Phase of dating. Alternatively, the next chapter addresses the situations when couples decide to move on in separate directions. It's important to note that both are okay as this is not a race to find a partner. It's a process that everyone goes through at their own pace.

Chapter Summary:

During and after your date, be sure to go back to your list and evaluate the date against your relationship goals. The key is to remember to be objective and if the situation presented does not meet your essentials and ideals, let them and yourself be free to move on. If your date points to a good match continue to communicate your expectations and goals openly and honestly in order to move forward.

The time spent between the A and B Phase of dating is crucial. It is frequently in this phase that people reveal their true colors and real truths. This can be scary and wonderful. It's important to allow your heart to keep pounding with hope and possibility whilst keeping your head thinking and learning about whether who they truly are can really work for you. Healthy evaluation can provide confidence in the potential of the relationship moving fully into the B Phase and, eventually, entering into the C Phase...the phase that represents commitment.

Assess as you go along by keeping an open mind and by being aware and curious. Go back to your list, embrace your longings and look reality in the eye whilst being excited at life and love's possibilities.

Chapter 9: Making the Right Decision for You

I hold it true, whate'er befall; I feel it, when I sorrow most;
'Tis better to have loved and lost than never to have loved at all.
- Albert Tennyson

If the first few dates don't feel right to you, it is time to let go and move on. This may bring about feelings of abandonment, rejection, disappointment, guilt and even loss. Intuitively, both parties may feel the beginning of getting to know each other will not lead to a desire to continue to see each other and inevitably, someone needs to "call it off" or drift away.

Coping with the need to move on is very difficult for many. It can be even more challenging because you're starting to make real connections with other people and even a few dates can create an early attachment and feelings of disappointment if things don't work out. Healthy, good choices that are compatible with your Essentials List are still what you are going for.

There are many ways to disconnect, healthy and unhealthy, polite and impolite, hurtful or truthful yet direct. How you do this is ultimately your call based on each situation. Letting go of a relationship can lead either one of you to the feelings of being disappointed or even rejected. But, as a wise friend of mine puts it quite simply, "If it's not right, it's wrong." Better for both of you to continue on your own way and to find other compatible mates...especially when your heart knows it is not right for you.

Rejection

"Rejection" is often an overused and even harsh word when used in this early phase of dating. How deeply hurt can you really feel if someone you have met once or only a few times decides this is not right for them? This is not a lifetime spent together. This is not years of a solid relationship or even marriage. It is only a short time of knowing someone in an unconventional way. Being totally insecure or deeply disappointed is not necessary. This is about your longings and desires and therefore it is important to realize that things may not work out with this particular person.

Just like in your career or any other aspect of your life, in dating you must have belief in yourself and develop a thick skin. Disappointment is a natural part of relationships. In this case, it's frequently more about the disappointment around the potential of what could have been. But if you start berating the other person or yourself, or experience a lapse in self-esteem as a result of a relationship not unfolding in the way you wanted it to, then I would suggest you spend more time on the Preparing Yourself Emotionally section so you can build up your confidence. In order to be in the beginning of a relationship you need to have a sense of positivity about yourself and your journey to find love. There needs to be a sense of flexibility, playfulness and mindfulness. Those are the qualities that will sustain you through challenging times. If someone choosing to not continue dating you makes you extremely sad or depressed, I find that this is a good time and opportunity to help people when they see me professionally. The goal is to feel empowered about your dating future. You don't control everything, just your reactions and it can be so helpful to reach out and get support when you need it.

Similarly, to be able to decide you can set boundaries and feel comfortable and entitled to say "no" to going to the next level is a sign of maturity and progress. You have to be able to do this when you know the person is not right for you. You are, after all, trying to choose what and who would be good for you and to do this, you need to be able to value these needs in yourself.

Do you feel slighted easily? Depending on how you answer this question will depend on how much of the Preparing Yourself Emotionally you need to go back and assess. Try not to feel slighted and know you can withstand setbacks. Be easy on yourself and don't look at it as a major or personal rejection since this person and you have only met a few times!

If you have abandonment issues they could emerge at this time. Feelings of disappointment and guilt can emerge at this time as can a sense of hopelessness, fear and lack of trust. Do not give up! Ironically, people can be so concerned about being said no to, that they don't consider that they have to be the one who says "no" to someone who is not right for them. Ultimately, establishing the ability to say no is about meeting your own needs and having the courage to attempt to choose appropriately for yourself. Keep in mind that the other person has the right to do the same with regards to you. Trust yourself and this process and you will find yourself able to say no to one person which will open a door to allow you to find someone who can be just what you have been yearning for! If you experience guilt or feel you cannot say no out of the fear of hurting someone, remember that you are hurting yourself by doing and being with someone that you are not attracted to emotionally or physically. Guilt feelings are often about the fear of hurting someone. A dose of guilt is fine if you intentionally set out to hurt someone by your behavior. In this case, it would be appropriate to feel accountable for your actions and apologize for hurting that person. Generally, though, hurting and being hurt are a part of life and not done to hurt or out of malice. Do not be hard on yourself for choosing what is best for you. Rather, trust that this is what needs to happen for you and the person you met. They will move on, as will you.

There are different levels of fear that come up for each person around letting go or being let go of. Depending on the length of the relationship and the unique insecurities of the individual partner, the intensity of hurt can vary from a small inconvenience to a monumental loss.

In the A Phase of dating, much of the emotions and fear around letting someone go is not as impactful as those who were in a committed, long-term relationship. However, it should not be discounted or disregarded as insignificant. Think about it more as not compromising on important values rather than an outright rejection of a person who may well be perfect for someone else at some other time. The unconscious process of finding and refinding a significant other based on early models can also help here. We spoke about this way of finding the familiar in the present before. After the date, you could reflect on what aspects of the person were familiar in a way that made you not want to further seek them out. What qualities do you feel you need to reconnect with that you are used to having from loved ones in your life? What qualities do you need to avoid this time around being more self-aware?

In ending a relationship, you are not there to accommodate the needs of another, especially if yours aren't being met. Have compassion for yourself for how hard it can be to nip something in the bud with an otherwise wonderful person because you feel or have discovered they are not right for you. And similarly, have compassion for yourself if they feel the same way. If it's not meant to be it can still be mined as a positive dating experience. Think of it as something that will allow you to learn more about yourself and relationships as a whole. And you can go forward with clarity.

As Erich Fromm, the psychoanalyst and social philosopher who explored the interaction between psychology and society says, "Immature love says: '*I love you because I need you.*' Mature love says '*I need you because I love you.*'" As you agreed to try to go for a love that works for you, trust yourself, the process and the unfolding of life and all its opportunities.

How long does this phase last?

A good rule of thumb is that the process of knowing someone can take anywhere from three to seven or eight months. It takes less time when people note the red flags and use their instincts to ask more questions. Practice and experience are important. As time goes on and the relationship starts feeling right to you both, you will become more comfortable with each other. This stage often leads to talking about exclusivity and the desire for a deeper connection that is starting to unfold that you both perceive. If this describes you, then you are gearing up for the B phase of *The ABCs of Dating*! This transition occurs when you feel things are "right" and you want to continue moving forward.

Chapter Summary:

Nobody likes to be either the person being let go of or the person doing the letting go. Rejection is too strong a word. It has too many negative associations and it is not relevant so early on. It's about choosing and making decisions. When both people are able to see letting one another go in order to be free to find the right person in a positive light, then it makes the separation much easier.

Early on in dating, after a few meetings, is when you will discover if you want to continue dating or not. This is your choice. People who are overly sensitive in the beginning phase of getting to know each other should evaluate why this is such a concern for them. These feelings and anxieties may occur later, too, if things do not proceed well. After all, *The ABCs of Dating* is about both the ups and downs of dating. Everyone has the right to make emotional choices if someone isn't right for them. It is a part of the process of forming solid relationships with the right people.

The bottom line is that choosing and letting go is not the same as "rejection" which is an exaggeration. Think about the words "Not meant to be," and what they mean to you. You can learn to feel great about your choices and even better about new beginnings. Anticipate another new beginning with enthusiasm.

Chapter 10: The 'B' Phase: Building Blocks of a Relationship

Now join your hands, and with your hands your hearts.
-William Shakespeare

Developing a Sense of Security and Stability

Congratulations! You have mutually decided to move forward giving this relationship a chance! Welcome to the B Phase of dating. The B Phase concepts are about the decision that you enjoy one another's company and that there is enough to work with to start building an ongoing exclusive relationship. You can be yourself and trust that the relationship is moving forward. There is a convergence and like-mindedness and a congruence of values and attraction. This phase feels good and if it continues because both people are interested in the ongoing and often fun process of becoming closer, can lead to the best of the B's...the Bonding.

The B Phase is still early enough in the relationship that you are continuing to learn about who your partner truly is. With all the work you have done on yourself and all the calm and necessary caution you have cultivated, you can appreciate who your partner is on a deeper level. As both of you continue to reveal more and more to each other, difficult issues from your respective pasts will or have been shared and addressed. Hopefully both of you are growing both individually and as a couple. You can recognize if and how your connection is being affected by these issues, and if so, work alone and together to become more of a unit.

Hopefully, all the red flags, up to now, have been

addressed and worked through and you are staying with this relationship, not out of desperation and neediness or fear, but because it's healthy and feels good. The middle part of a relationship comes in the B Phase, which means moving towards the harmony of middle stages. In this phase, you will feel more relaxed and comfortable with someone who was once a stranger but is now becoming a more significant part of your life.

However, I have to point out that the beginning of the B Phase still implies that the proverbial buyer should beware. You still need to stay balanced, have belief in the relationship from time spent together and see if it feels like there is a healthy attachment developing. After these are met, you can truly dive into the B Phase.

The B Phase of Dating Key Words:
- Bonding
- Balance
- Boundaries
- Behavior
- Belief
- Breathing

Just like the A Phase, consider these words and what they mean to you. For example, *Boundaries* have varied meanings for each person. *Behavior* is another word that has varying degrees of latitude as to what's acceptable and what is not. Being clear with each area of the B Phase and these terms will help you transition from the A Phase to the B Phase more readily. Below are the words with their descriptions; however, you may want to pull out your notebook and write down your own interpretations as well.

- *Bonding* means that the two of you are developing a connection between you that goes deeper. You are sharing personal things with one another, more activities, feelings and thoughts that continue to strengthen the relationship, build trust and allow a solid connection to form. You are developing an identity as a couple with fun activities, quirks and your own narrative of your shared new life together with emotional and sexual intimacy developing. This makes this time and stage in your relationship feel unique and special to you both.
- *Balance* is a key element in the functioning of a relationship. When two people can find a healthy balance between work, personal life and the relationship, is when progress is being made. With great balance comes great stability. Think of walking on a balancing beam. To do it, you need both strength and stability, otherwise you might fall. It takes a few discussions to work through finding that balance that works for the relationship and both of you as individuals. Keep the discussions open and honest and you will find balance. Another aspect of Balance also refers to the interplay of alone versus couple time. It's the dance of intimacy and togetherness versus separation that each couple has to figure out for themselves and negotiate well. This interweaving of the personal need for space and the needs for togetherness as a couple, begins more in earnest in the B phase of dating and continues all the way through co-creating a functional and wonderful relationship.

- *Boundaries*, and their definition, are a key part of creating balance in a relationship. Everyone has personal needs that require boundaries to feel safe. Being open with your partner early on about the boundaries of the relationship will reduce problems down the road. Defining the boundaries of what you need personally in order to make the relationship work should be done with compassion and directness. For instance, do you have a boundary as to how many past significant others you are still close to? Does your partner? Do you have a boundary in terms of how many evenings you need on your own or with your own friends? If you are divorced with children, do you have a boundary that you spend alone time without your new significant other with your children? Do you have the boundary that you too at times want to be included? It's complex but interesting to navigate. You both want to be able to set your boundaries and learn about and respect your partner in an open and honest way.
- *Behavior* can be something that frequently shifts and reveals itself in the B Phase of the relationship. For example, you are no longer just meeting for dinner or coffee and feeling like you are on your best behavior or show only qualities you want revealed. You are now relaxing more and spending time together in natural lifestyle settings, such as at home, which should feel comfortable and intimate. Whether going to one another's homes or having weekend getaways, the tides have changed to include more than just an hour or two over a meal. A person starts to show their true colors in these regular settings,

and in the early part of the B Phase, you will learn a lot more about your partner than what was possible before. It's a great way to start to share your true self and the day to day events of life and feel more connected throughout the week.

- *Belief.* In the B Phase of the relationship you've transitioned from hope to *belief.* You have reasons to believe you are in a healthy and good relationship. You reassure one another that the relationship is continuing and you both agree you want it to. Some of this comes through discussions and some of it is just the feeling you have when you know you are with the right person.
- *Breathing* easily in a relationship shows you that the anxiety is gone and the feelings of security and comfort have settled in. Being in a phase of a relationship where the initial activity has settled into a routine allows you to breathe normally and effortlessly and enjoy the relationship for where it is right now. Emotional safety and peacefulness are great feelings.

Sharing and Enjoying the Mundane

This is an important transition. Early-on dating might mean that you looked your best all the time and the process of discovery to get to this B stage took a great deal of time, activities and many social arrangements. Now that you are in this next phase, you can loosen up, share and enjoy the mundane regular aspects of life. Doing laundry, washing the car or going to the supermarket together can be great opportunities to just experience the simple pleasures of life. It's about being together and not always in glamorous places.

Enjoying life's daily chores and simplicity and finding pleasure in the day-to-day experience is part of enriching an intimate relationship. Many people want to be able to skip right to the B Phase or C Phase of a relationship without doing the work to arrive there. By taking the time to get here the right way can make all the difference in the world. Arriving at the place where mundane is considered a part of normalcy means you've arrived at a new level of your relationship. It's not about the "dates" anymore. There already is the chance to look back at the nervousness and excitement of what the heart was feeling on those first few early dates. A sense of perspective will develop and, as the early issues have been worked through, it can be an exciting time to begin to look to the future. The B Phase is often a time when you start to meet your partner's friends and family and to think ahead, start sharing more interests and developing new ones as a couple.

Discovering Compatibility

Discovering compatibility is where people often learn that they enjoy similar things as a part of daily routines. Or they discover that their partner is open to learning and being exposed to new experiences, activities and friendships. For instance, it may give you both joy to enjoy a quiet Sunday morning reading the newspaper and making breakfast. Either way, whether similar or different, you are discovering areas of compatibility that create excitement, that comfortable feeling of security and a developing sense of love. It's often a time when the words "I love you" pop out without thought. It's often a wonderful and special moment to both people to verbalize what they have been feeling.

The Dance of Intimacy

In the B Phase, it is important to create balance between your individual needs, the needs of your partner and the needs of the relationship.

I like to think of a relationship as two intersecting circles. It is the dance of togetherness versus individuality and each couple is unique in determining what amount of intersection of circles exists for them and what percentage of alone time works for their union. It's again looking at the intimacy of what each of you needs and communicating about your differences directly and openly.

It's a time for working through conflicts, or coping together as new things crop up that may not have emerged before. It can still be a time of surprises and fears but also excitement. There may be issues that have not been shared as you or your partner may have tried to foster more intimacy, bonding and trust before addressing them in conversation. It's a time of dealing with more of the realities of daily life, which hopefully has improved because of this connection that is developing and the comfort of another in your life.

Dr. Seuss said, "*You know you're in love when you can't fall asleep because reality is finally better than your dreams.*" Dr. Seuss was a genius.

Chapter Summary:

Most people in the A Phase of a relationship are excited to move forward into the B Phase. If you have gone through the A Phase you have likely been spending time weeding out the wrong people and finally meeting the right one. In this case, the B Phase is a wonderful phase to be in. The anxiety that comes with newness is diminishing and is replaced with positive feelings that the relationship is right and moving ahead. Bonding, balance, belief and boundaries are all congruent parts of this phase making the relationship work so that you can move more readily into the C Phase, that of Commitment.

Chapter 11: C's: 'C' is for Commitment

For through this world we walk together Near or Far
Together we are in soul and heart
And may all our days be filled with quintessential pleasures
—From Quintessential Pleasures by William Loyd Brown

A Deepening of the Relationship

All this hard work and due diligence applying the process of *The ABCs of Dating* book outline has led you both to the point of wanting to deepen your relationship. Now you will work out together what this means and entails. It can mean moving in together, or an engagement and marriage or whatever it is that both of you ultimately longed for. This phase often goes smoothly as you have been mindful, present and clear and continued to ask questions. Love, compatibility and commitment should not come as a surprise now. Many people long for this stage and do not realize all that may have gone into developing to this point. Mutually, you have arrived at your own identities as individuals and forged one as a couple as well. In the C phase of *The ABCs of Dating*, it is your work as a committed couple to keep love alive and attraction thriving.

Of course, this is just another beginning as maintaining intimacy, connectedness, fun, sexuality and similar values and goals is under constantly shifting ground. Remember that this is what you wanted and strived for! Being positive and having gratitude for having made a great choice will be what helps you continue to develop the relationship with maturity, depth and longevity.

There will be a constant interplay of those intersecting circles. Couples have to work hard to be sure that what they need in terms of this balance is working and if it changes, they need to have the skills to negotiate, communicate fairly and adapt with their significant other. This is the work of all committed and healthy relationships: appreciating and recognizing what you have established and maintaining intimacy, trust and communication.

Words to associate with the C Phase of Dating:
- Commitment
- Choice
- Communication
- Connection
- Content
- Contentment
- Contrast
- Courtesy
- Courage
- Celebration

The commitment to being in a relationship, which includes sharing similar goals, values and dreams, makes you feel like a community of two, a family and a true couple. There may be a desire for a long-term marriage or partnership that is mutually discussed well before this phase. Thus the desire for commitment should not be a surprise if you have been talking, sharing and listening. However, for many, commitment is still a scary word and the idea of long-term pledges are frightening to many. Often, this is the time where previous self-reflection and work on oneself will truly pay off. There is more excitement and joy about sharing than there is apprehension or the feeling that there is no other choice but to go forward. It is a chance where love and healthy attachment overcome fears around commitment. These fears may be about feelings of enmeshment or loss of self or time for oneself, and they are always interplaying in your dynamic relationship. Let's discuss these words and aspects of this new and deepening level of the relationship in more detail:

Commitment

Commitment is the foundation of the C Phase of dating. You are at the point of being in a committed and, most likely, an exclusive relationship. Sexuality, monogamy and life goals have been discussed and recognized as mutually desired. The commitment to continue on with your existing relationship stems from this connection.

Choice

You are making a choice, based on deep longings, similar goals and all the work you did in the A Phase. Making real choices helps when conflicts do arise, as they do in all committed relationships. When you make a choice about this relationship, mindfully and with a full and open heart and clear vision, then it is a lot easier to tolerate the ups and downs that "normal" committed relationships have. People are complex and relationships can be challenging and mystifying. There is no utopia but with choices made from a place of love, commitment and respect, all committed relationships can endure and thrive.

If you do your best with the recognition that you chose this connection, it can help in hard times. There should be more love than ambivalence or anger. Hopefully, you would not have made this commitment if you had not been desirous of it before arriving at this part of your journey to find love. But it is an ongoing journey, not a one stop destination.

Communication

In *The ABCs of Dating*, communication is stressed. It's not always easy to listen and hear another's point of view. Couples can feel polarized at times and conflicts occur. How deeply rooted they are has a lot to do with previous communication. Are there still huge surprises? Each of you should still have a thriving individual identity. There is the intactness of the couple to uphold for sure but there is also the need for individual growth. The parameters of this are set and reset as in that dance of intimacy. The overlaying circles may be realigned; however, the two circles do have to intersect and it is up to both of you to communicate what is the middle of that intersection. A healthy, committed relationship is comprised of mutual interests, quality time together, sexuality and playfulness, similar interests and interaction with friends and family. There is space outside the intersection where each of the couple ought to be utilizing their "alone" time creatively and in service to themselves. What makes an individual happy will impact the relationship. What is missing in the intersecting parts will impact the happiness as well.

For instance, if one of you is miserable in your career and detests your day at work, you may return miserable to your relationship and it will not feel that the "intersecting of circles," that essential place for a couple to share is being nurtured. There should be dialogue about maintaining respect and communicating your feelings to your loved one. Do you greet each other with a smile, or walk through the door grimacing and complaining? Are you texting and barely looking up from your laptop when your partner walks in the door? There exists both positive and negative communication and it is important as a couple to decide what works for you both and try to follow and sustain paths towards intimacy and connection.

Mother Teresa states, *"Let us always meet each other with a smile, for the smile is the beginning of love."* It's important to share, to communicate about your days. It is fine to not have felt happy that day, but the person who is listening to you is not an extension of yourself. Separation and individuation is what you have worked on.

Remember your communication can always be adjusted and worked on so that it allows you the best reception and the most amount of nurturing in return. And people can communicate according to what their compatibility has indicated. If both need a great deal of daily interaction and communication, then be sure to remember this. A smile, a loving text, a thoughtful gesture, a funny note and sense of humor allow you on a daily basis to enjoy your commitment and honor this relationship with someone you've found that is simpatico.

To commit to love should be ever-present, not a onetime action or conversation. It should be a daily communication about your happiness, the correctness of your choice and a celebration of love.

Connection

A feeling of connection with another or others is important to ones wellbeing. To share, to have empathy, to connect, makes many people feel healed and not alone. To others, connection may be more troubling. In an intimate relationship, one needs to feel connected emotionally and physically. Affection helps people do just that. Ingrid Bergman stated that *"A kiss is a lovely trick designed by nature to stop speech when words become superfluous."* The physical attraction, the like-mindedness and differences are all points where people can find ways to connect and feel connected in a powerful way.

Content

This is a time to remember your dating narrative and story: your dates, meetings and the beginning of your conversations where you enjoyed getting to know each other. The content of these conversations was one of the factors that made you want to continue the relationship. And so now that you are in this place of commitment, is the content still interesting? Are you both making the effort to keep it so? Do you include your loved one in your interests and passions and do you feel enlivened by theirs? The content of day to day life in a relationship is for you to fill in and it needs to work and be worked on. Some people find that the little and fun relationship rituals that they have created during the B Phase of *The ABCs of Dating* are providing content and context for their relationship to continue feeling alive in this commitment phase. As plants need watering and care, so does the fabric and content of any relationship. Are you in a lull as a couple or are you making the effort to do the interesting things you did together and remembering what drew you together? Are you always out and about with no "down" time to just be and relax? Do you cook together or listen to music? Is your sex life still vibrant and are you committed to keep it so? These are a few examples of ways to spend quality day to day time together in the relationship you create. There are many strategies and helpful ways to build a better intimate relationship and more fun together.

The day to day rhythm of a relationship needs to be the heartbeat of the relationship. The base line togetherness should be pleasurable and then one can add or subtract to the content of keeping it so.

Contentment

In the C phase of *The ABCs of Dating*, contentment does describe the feeling of no longer searching and striving. There is often gratitude for the blessings of sharing one's life with another who truly cares and through weathering the ups and the downs of daily life. There is often a peacefulness that comes from the emotional safety that this relationship you have created together provides. And it's fine to count one's blessings about being in a committed and caring relationship. It's blending sexuality and emotional togetherness in a commitment you both cherish.

Contrast

All relationships are different and may have had very different trajectories. There is no way to contrast an absolute. There should be a contrast between how you now feel, being in this phase of an evolving relationship and the way you felt before being in a close relationship. There are always the differences in temperament, personality and style in couples. There are vastly contrasting styles of communication often, yet a deep compatibility and commitment that work. Rumi said, "What you seek is seeking you." This statement could refer to the concept of finding in the present all the best of what had been the earliest blueprints of love, connection and intimacy that you experienced in childhood. The familiar can return in ways that work. And if there was no map you wanted to follow or could follow, you can do the work to journey to find what now really works for you in the choice you make in the present.

Courtesy

There is the kindness and courtesy of affording the committed relationship the same ground rules as earlier on when first meeting. Familiarity should not breed contempt! Politeness, kindness, courtesy and putting the relationship above work or friendships are issues to address and attempt to uphold and preserve. As life is never perfect and many pressures occur from the outside that make demands and put pressure on you as a couple, remember to uphold the benefits of what you are building in this commitment phase of your relationship and treat the relationship with the respect and courtesy it deserves. It is like a flower and to blossom, it needs to be attended to, valued and mutually cared for.

Courage

It does take courage to have gotten to this point. It takes courage to rise and fall and rise again! There are real life challenges and feelings to address. Life does not occur in a bubble and couples are not exempt from internal and external challenges. Many may find safety in being a couple and are grateful. However, there is always courage needed to support, nurture and emotionally provide for your loved one through thick and thin. Courage can be seen in many couples enduring hardship. Have courage to continue and rely on your love to help overcome loss, hardship and the vicissitudes of life.

As Lao Tzu says, *"Being deeply loved by someone gives you strength, while loving someone deeply gives you courage."*

Celebration

It's important for couples moving into committed relationships to have pride in their growth, from the beginning, through the middle B phase, to the beginning of a commitment. Celebration of this commitment to continuing a happy relationship is a meaningful part of this phase. It's important to celebrate milestones, to reflect, laugh and share memories and to continue to create new ones together. Living with love is a celebration of your lives together.

Enjoy and celebrate your accomplishments, your hard work and your happiness in life's adventures. This is about your dreams coming true! So own this amazing achievement and celebrate! Love is the greatest and purest truth and brings the greatest solace and happiness to many.

As John Lennon sang:
And in the end
The love you take
Is equal to the love you make.

Chapter 12: Words to Date (and Live) By

The ABCs of Dating was meant to inspire you in your quest for love. Hopefully, you have grown no matter the outcome in your dating quest and your readiness and longings have been assessed by yourself on a deep level. Ultimately, you are listening to your own truth and need to be and feel worthy.

Do not be afraid of living well and of loving fully. It starts with you... and your beliefs and ability to overcome fear, to achieve your dreams and to live with LOVE.

So many people are simply afraid. They are gripped by the fear that they are not good enough. That is not true. You are.

Finding and nurturing a deep and real loving relationship with another person is really just the beginning of a new phase in life where love and respect become infused in your day to day living. Love emanates from those relationships and can't help but to inform our broader world. But what's important to remember is that it is your world. You matter, first and foremost, and from this place you can find love and you can sustain love. To wake to a new day in that place is one of life's greatest gifts.

The real surprise comes when you get there and realize that it is more than a new beginning, it is the only way the world at large can thrive and flourish. To love is simply human. To paraphrase the great Nelson Mandela *...love comes naturally to the human heart.*

Do not be afraid of being who you authentically are and feel good and, yes, proud of your best qualities. Many people say that the best thing about being in love with the right person is that they are able to fully be themselves and to allow the person they love to be who they are, without judgments.

Your insecurities are a part of you...as they are a part of all of us. In everyone is the power to shine and be their best selves, not based on external achievements alone but on inner truths and personal accomplishments. Everyone has a different journey. Nelson Mandela has been attributed to sharing a speech in his inaugural address from Marianne Williamson's book "Return to Love." Although he didn't actually use the passage, I'm sure he would deeply understand and appreciate it.

I wish to honor Nelson Mandela for putting love over hate and for being a beacon of light and love. *"And as we let our own light shine, we unconsciously give other people permission to do the same.*

As we are liberated from our own fear, our presence automatically liberates others."

Some *ABCs of Dating* Ground Rules

- Honest communication is essential.
- Ask questions when getting to know someone and don't "guess" what you think the answer is or anticipate someone else's answers.
- Avoid generalizations which are usually negative and often wrong. "All men think or want this," "All women are the same" etc. Men and women are different from each other in many ways, but all of them belong under the species "human beings." Resist assumptions and projections. Treat each person as the unique individual they are and get to know them by asking questions and spending time together.
- Your partner doesn't have to have the same individual life goals as you but you both should be compatible in terms of lifestyle and values. Readiness to be in an intimate relationship is a prerequisite to moving forward together.
- There should be a good fit in terms of what you both want out of life as a couple and unconsciously, a real connection between you that is positive and brings out the best in both of you.
- Timing is important. The right person at the right time of readiness to be in a mature relationship is likely to yield positive results.
- Attraction both physical and emotional is an essential. You are not being superficial to need to enjoy these components. They are foundational to many and need to be honored.
- You should feel comfortable and satisfied with your sexual compatibility. It should feel alive and special to you both throughout the relationship and evolve for

the better with time. Attraction, lust, romance, sensuality and passion are here to stay! Make that so for yourself and your partner.
- Being open to accommodate and compromise is important, but never at the expense of your own wellbeing.
- Trust your instincts and be curious and open to learning about yourself and others.
- Deal with your own insecurities and remember you need to like yourself and feel worthy of love to love another more truly.
- Find interest in your own life and in creating a viable community for yourself. It'll feel much more natural and comfortable to socialize.
- Great dating always comes from being authentically YOU!

Final Thoughts

Even though these are my final thoughts, reading *The ABCs of Dating* should be a beginning for you. All relationships take the proverbial work. Enjoy the process of discovery and have faith in the challenging times. Remember to hold onto all the beauty that brought you together as you sustain your commitment.

Avoid confusion that can come from getting wrapped up in statistics and other people's experiences. Look at positive role models and decide proactively for yourself what you wish for and try hard to create it. There is objective reality, but there is your own subjective experience: go for what you want in the here and the now. Believe in your longings for love and the process of looking for that special connection. Have fun and faith in yourself and in others looking for love. Sooner or later, you two will find each other and will know it is "right." Keep adding to your list and making your dreams for dating and love fun, enticing, creative, happy and inspired.

I hope you will read and re-read *The ABCs of Dating* and feel inspired to venture out into the world of dating. Be sure to find belief in yourself and faith in life's possibilities. Each phase of dating mirrors all the ups and downs of life. You are evolving as is love. Love is worth embarking on for the joy of connection to yourself, the world and that special other that is out there for you to find and to love.

To Love, For Love, With Love

About the Author

Brenda A. Lewis, LCSW, is a New York City based psychotherapist with over two decades of experience in private practice. Her creative strategies, outlined here in *The ABCs of Dating*, have helped many men and women struggling in the area of relationships and complex dating issues. She has led many singles to find new meaning in their quest for love. Couples who have worked with Brenda have found happiness and connectedness within their relationships and marriages. In addition to general therapy, she deals with sexual and intimacy issues in individuals and couples and is experienced at addressing themes of non-functioning elements within relationships to empower positive change. Working with all ages and different cultures and backgrounds, she is highly adept at understanding and illuminating the dynamics of the power of love.